Contents

The Storyteller's Cornucopia

2nd Edition

Cathie Hilterbran Cooper

Fort Atkinson, Wisconsin

Published by Alleyside Press, an imprint of Highsmith Press LLC
Highsmith Press
W5527 Highway 106
P.O. Box 800
Fort Atkinson, Wisconsin 53538-0800
1-800-558-2110

© Cathie Hilterbran Cooper, 1998
Cover design: Frank Neu

The paper used in this publication meets the minimum requirements of American National Standard for Information Science — Permanence of Paper for Printed Library Material. ANSI/NISO Z39.48-1992.

Library of Congress Cataloging in Publication
    Cooper, Cathie Hilterbran, 1953-
      The storyteller's cornucopia / Cathie Hilterbran Cooper. –2nd
    ed.
      Includes bibliographical references (p)
      ISBN 1-59750-025-0 (soft : alk. paper)
      1. Storytelling. 2. Early childhood education–Activity programs.
    3. Teaching00Aids and devices. I. Title.
    LB1042.C487 1998
      027.62 ' 51–dc21   98-39884
                                                                        CIP

Introduction to Storytelling

Storytelling is an artform that can be traced from its beginnings in preliterate society to its current revival of interest. Isak Dinesen once wrote that "Stories have been told as long as speech has existed, and sans stories, the human race would have perished, as it would have perished sans water."[1] While the purpose and conditions vary in different times and cultures, storytelling fulfills the same basic needs for all people. Early storytellers were viewed with almost mystic awe and served a vital function in society. They reported news, shared experiences, ideas and values, served as entertainers, and became keepers of cultures. Ancient storytellers were often charged with teaching social and moral values as well as training children in the art of listening, interpreting and telling. The first professional storytellers were bards who sang and recited stories and histories to their listeners.

With the invention of the printing press, scholars began to publish these stories and the oral tradition of storytelling diminished to a form of entertainment. During the latter half of the nineteenth century and the early twentieth century, many social movements and changes in attitudes toward children continued to revive interest in storytelling. The introduction of kindergarten in public schools, establishment of playgrounds and settlement houses, and the founding of the Boy Scouts and Girl Scouts are a few of the events that resulted in an increased interest in providing organized formal presentations of stories to children.

Storytelling has long been an accepted practice in public library children's departments. In 1896 Anne Carroll Moore started informal story hours at the Pratt Institute in Brooklyn. When Moore became the first Superintendent of Work with Children with the New York Public Library system in 1907, she was responsible for the development of regular story hour programs at the library. Moore brought Anna Cogswell Tyler to the system to establish a formal storytelling program. By 1909 the program was in progress, and Tyler became the first supervisor of storytelling for the library. Another early advocate of story hours in libraries was Frances Jenkins Olcott, head of the children's department at the Carnegie Library of Pittsburgh. Together with professional storytellers Marie Shedlock and Gudrun Thorne-Thomsen (from the Chicago area), these women were responsible for the development and growth of storytelling sessions in children's rooms in public libraries across the country. They believed that storytelling was the best way to motivate children to read and that by using oral literature they could guide children to the printed word.

For much of the twentieth century, storytelling was regarded as an activity to use with children. However, by the early 1970s, adults began to reclaim storytelling for themselves. In 1973, Jimmy Neil Smith started a storytelling festival in Jonesborough, Tennessee. Nearly 300 people attended the first festival and swapped stories. Today the annual festival draws thousands of storytellers during the first week of October. Smith founded the National Storytellers Association (NSA), which now has over 8,000 members from around the world. NSA is only one of dozens of groups that promote storytellers. Formal workshops, seminars and college courses have emerged from this revival of an ancient tradition. Not since the Middle Ages has there been so many people who practice the art of storytelling.

A large portion of our daily conversation consists of stories and anecdotes which makes all of us storytellers in one sense of the word. Although professionally trained storytellers are polished and experienced in their presentations, anyone who is willing to invest time and energy into learning some simple techniques can become a successful storyteller. Storytelling is important for a number of reasons, not the least of which is that it is a pleasurable experience for both the speaker and the listener and it develops a bond between the two. There is no doubt that storytelling delights and entertains, but it can also be used as a valuable teaching tool.

Storytelling:

- encourages appreciation and sharing of the ancient art form of storytelling;
- teaches new ideas and the value systems of other cultures and a better understanding of our own;
- expands language skills and encourages language development;
- stimulates and strengthens creativity and colors the imagination;
- helps children to develop listening skills and increased attention spans;
- encourages children to read and expands a child's exposure to literature;
- helps students to develop better sequencing skills and encourages recall and memory skills;

But most of all, it is <u>fun</u>! both for the storyteller and the listener.

Selecting a Story

Every storyteller develops criteria in selecting a story. The following considerations are useful guidelines when choosing a story, but they are not the only criteria for story selection.

Appeal to the Storyteller

Appeal is the most important consideration in selecting a story. If the storyteller likes a story, then the children will probably like it. Your initial spontaneous reaction to a story is generally right. If you like a story, then it shows in your voice, mannerisms, and method of presentation. If a story is not appealing to the storyteller, then this lack of interest will show in the storyteller's voice and presentation.

The Storyteller's Limitations

The storyteller must consider what method of presentation to use, the length of the story, the location of the story, and what props will be needed.

Audience

When choosing a story, consider the age level of the audience. The type of story that you select for preschoolers is different from the type that you select for third graders. If you have to cover a broad age spectrum, then choose a story for the upper age bracket.

In addition to age, consider the attention span of the audience. The younger the child, the shorter the attention span will be. After carefully considering the age and attention span of the children, you may need to adapt a complex story line to fit children's needs. For preschoolers (ages 3 to 5), use simple stories, songs, and rhymes because your main goal is to dispense information and to develop an appreciation for the written word and illustrations. Primary age children (ages 6 to 8) are more active listeners with longer attention spans and a greater capability to understand more complex plots and language. For middle grade children (ages 8 to 12), story programs can be more formal and traditional. This age group can better appreciate and understand the longer folktales and myths.

Consider the time span you will have. In most schools, students visit the library for a limited time period that includes both story time and book browsing time. For example, I have kindergarten classes once a week for fifteen to twenty minutes. During that time, I usually tell a story and allow the students five to ten minutes to select books to take home. This short time period limits the number and type of stories that I can use with the children.

Elements of a Good Story

The two most important elements of a good story are:

Familiar Conditions

A good story should be one in which the setting and characters are easily identified by the children. Consider the proposed audience and whether they are familiar with the concepts, settings, and characters in the story. Telling a story about urban life to a group of children who have never seen a skyscraper may require some adaptation by the storyteller. Of course, with older children, the setting and characters can be more complex and imaginative.

The Unusual or Surprise Ending

Nothing is more fun than a surprise ending. Although most stories follow a set formula, it is fun for children to find a surprise on the last page. Just as adults enjoy trying to second-guess the writers of whodunits, children like to find the unexpected or unusual in a story. This concept is evident from the popularity of psychological thrillers and adventure stories on both television and in movie theaters.

Form of a Good Story

A good story follows certain criteria in the presentation of the plot, characters, and setting, including the following:

Introduction

The story needs a short but arresting introduction to prepare the reader for the plot. The introduction establishes the setting and presents the main characters for the reader or the listener.

Central Plot

A clear-cut plot makes a good story. The direct development of one sequential plot uncluttered with secondary plot lines makes the story easy to follow and to tell. Literary techniques such as flashbacks and stream of consciousness are too complex for children's stories. Simplicity is also the key to characters in the story. Although it is important for the characters to be interesting, colorful, and believable, it is best to keep the cast of major characters to a small number. Remember, you are telling a children's story not the plot of a complex multigenerational novel.

Climax

The action in the story should build up to one central climax. A good story has action and suspenseful events that build toward the climax and in the process holds the attention of the reader. Choose a story that has action and suspense. In stories for very young children (toddler story hours), rhythm and repetitive language replace the action and suspense plot line in stories for older children.

Resolution

The story should have a resolution of the plot following the climax. The resolution should be brief and clear like the introduction.

Aftermath

The story should leave the reader or listener with a sense of satisfaction. You should feel that the plot line has been resolved and that the characters are complete.

Digression and Description

A good story should not include too much digression from the central plot or too much narrative description. For read-alouds, a lot of conversation between characters makes it difficult for the listener to follow the plot. There should be enough conversation to make the story lively, but not enough to distract from the action.

Language

A good plot needs to have strong simple language with lots of action verbs. The language should match the style and nature of the story, and the words should create sensory images and feelings in the listener. Rhythmic language makes it easy for the listener to follow the action of the plot. Repetitive phrases and words heighten attentiveness to the story. Rhythm and repetitive phrases are especially effective with younger children.

Universal Subject Matter

The subject matter should have universal appeal to a wide range of age levels and should deal with easily identifiable concepts such as family, sibling relations, and school life.

Sources and Types of Stories

When choosing a story to tell, you are confronted by a wide realm of possibilities, from real to imaginary, old to new, and animal stories to fairy tales. The list is endless and includes both narrative and nonnarrative sources.

Folktales and fairy tales are the first choices for many beginners and are especially good for traditional storytelling. These tales are usually stories that have been handed down through the generations and range from repetitive tales (*Three Little Bears*) and beast tales (*Bremen Town Musicians*) to nonsense tales (*Three Sillies*) and nursery tales (*Cinderella*).

Myths and legends are also particularly good for traditional storytelling. Legends from the past such as those about Robin Hood and King Arthur are widely accepted as being based in truth but are questioned in the true historical sense. A myth is a legendary story widely used to explain a belief or idea.

Epics, or sagas, are a third type of story easily adapted to traditional storytelling. These stories deal with some heroic act or deed and are told with a sense of stately dignity and pride.

Imaginative tales are stories that range from the ridiculous and absurd (Betty MacDonald's *Mrs.*

Piggle Wiggle and Miguel Cervantes' *Don Quixote*) to the truly farfetched (Robert O'Brien's *Mrs. Frisby and the Rats of NIMH* and C. S. Lewis' *The Lion, the Witch and the Wardrobe*).

Modern tales are those stories that have become popular during the past hundred years. Modern tales include humorous stories such as P. L. Travers' *Mary Poppins* and nature and animal stories such as Robert McCloskey's *Make Way for Ducklings* and E. B. White's *Charlotte's Web*.

Picture books are an excellent source of tales to read aloud or to adapt to a puppet, flannelboard, or participation type of storytelling presentation. Many picture books such as Maurice Sendak's *Where the Wild Things Are* and Dr. Seuss' *The Cat in the Hat* have become contemporary classics that will probably remain popular with many generations of readers.

A number of nonnarrative materials are also useful in story programs. For example, riddles, tongue twisters, proverbs, jokes, word games, autograph and skip rope rhymes, and string and folk games can be used to enhance and supplement a story program.

Always be certain to attribute the source of your story. It is important to give proper credit to the author or adapter of a story you are using, and to respect copyright laws and regulations. As a librarian or teacher, you may make "fair use" of a story for educational purposes, but if you are using a copyrighted work in a paid public performance or broadcast, you must obtain the copyright holder's permission. If you have a question about what constitutes fair use, contact the publisher of the work you are using.

Preparation

Some basic tips to use for preparing for a storytelling session include:

Learn the Plot and Sequence

The first time that you read a story, read it aloud and time the reading. There will be some time discrepancies between a word-for-word read-aloud and the retelling of a story, but the time discrepancies should be minor. Practice in front of anyone who will listen, and if no one will listen, then practice alone. Read the story aloud several times to get a feel for the plot, characters, and language. Everyone develops a method of preparing for telling stories. Use whatever method works best for you and makes you feel comfortable. Storytellers choose a variety of

ways to help them learn stories, including the following:

Audiotapes—Some people find that reading the story aloud and recording the reading is helpful. Do not be discouraged the first time that you record your voice. Audiotapes will highlight imperfections of voice and timing.

Videotapes—Videotaping captures facial mannerisms, unnecessary gestures, and imperfections in voice and timing. The first time that you videotape yourself can be an uncomfortable experience, so do not become discouraged.

Mirrors and practice sessions—One of the best methods for practicing aloud and catching distracting gestures and mannerisms is to rehearse in front of a mirror. As a beginning storyteller, I spent a lot of time talking to the bathroom mirror and rehearsing stories. Practice the story anywhere—while weeding the garden, cooking, ironing, showering, driving, or even trying to go to sleep at night. The keyword is practice, wherever you feel most comfortable.

Other visual devices—For those who are visual rather than auditory learners, a number of techniques can be used to help you to learn a story.

Typing a story can help to create a carbon copy of it in the mind. This technique is especially helpful for flannelboard and puppet presentations. By typing the story, you can gain a sense of the sequence of the plot. You can use the typed copy to make notes on which flannelboard figures should be put up or taken off of the board at various points in the story and to make notes on the types and number of figures needed for a story.

Preparing either a formal or informal outline can also serve as a memory refresher. Outlining the action and the characters ingrains the story on the mind.

Cue cards also serve as a means of refreshing the memory about a story. Use 4"x6" index cards, and write some basic information about the story including the author, title, setting, major characters, and plot sequence. Preparing cue cards is a good way to keep a file on when, where, and how you used a story.

Choreographing a story also facilitates memorization, and reviewing a story and marking it to indicate place, timing, and voice changes can enhance recall of the plot and characters.

Absorb the Atmosphere of the Story

Become familiar with the setting of the story, especially if you are telling a folktale. Visualize and mentally recreate the story with all of its tastes, smells, sounds, and colors.

Visualize the Characters and the Setting

Be able to visualize the characters. How is a character dressed? What are his or her mannerisms? What character traits does he or she have? Is the character greedy, gentle, timid, loud, or happy? Picture the character. Is the character short or tall or fat or thin? How does the character speak? A character such as the emperor in *The Emperor's New Clothes* would speak in a pompous overbearing manner, while the inchworm in Leo Lionni's *Inch by Inch* would be shy and quiet. Where does the story take place? In the country, a zoo, or a jungle? During what season does it take place? What about the weather? Is it hot, cold, or snowy? Become involved with the characters and the setting. Know the characters as if they were your closest friends and the setting as if it were your own neighborhood or your favorite park. Being familiar with the characters and setting is especially important if you are using the traditional storytelling methods rather than a read-aloud style.

Become Familiar with the Sequence of Events and the Plot

Remember when and how events take place in a story, especially in repetitive and cumulative tales in which one bit of action builds on another.

Memorize the Story or Learn Keywords and Key Phrases

To memorize or not to memorize depends on the storyteller and the story. You may choose (1) to learn keywords and key phrases that occur over and over again such as "It's only fair" from *The Five Chinese Brothers* by Claire Hutchet Bishop and Kurt Wiese, or (2) to memorize the entire story word for word. Memorization is especially useful for short cumulative tales such as *The House that Jack Built* and Jack Kent's *The Fat Cat*.

Control Body Action

You need to prepare yourself for storytelling by eliminating any unnecessary gestures and distracting mannerisms. Gimmicks and practiced gestures are not needed to convey the story to the listener. The story is enough. A storyteller interprets and expresses the actions and views of the characters, but he or she does not become the character in the way that an actor would.

Analyze and Adapt Stories for Telling

When choosing a story, the storyteller analyzes it and sometimes adapts it for telling. Some stories lend themselves well to adaptation, especially those in which a complex plot can be condensed and edited for a one-time story program. When deciding to adapt or to edit a story, there are several options open to the storyteller. You may choose to (1) change the story from the first person to the third person or vice versa; (2) delete some minor characters, plot incidents, details, and descriptions that are not vital to the central story; (3) change narration to dialogue or vice versa; or even (4) rearrange some plot incidents for a smoother retelling.

If you are telling a story with complex or unfamiliar words or events, consider changing or adapting the word or event to one that is more familiar and tangible to the age level of your audience. However, do not spend time on a vocabulary lesson of unfamiliar words. The first time the word occurs in a story, use it as it appears. If your audience looks puzzled or asks for its meaning, just substitute a synonym the next time the word occurs. You might even consider alternating the original word and the synonym as you tell the story. Children are adept at determining the meanings of unfamiliar words by using contextual clues.

Hans Christian Anderson's *The Snow Queen* is a good example of a story that might be too long and complex to use with a group of preschoolers but that can be tailored for such a group. By condensing the plot, eliminating minor characters, and simplifying the language, the story can be successfully adapted for use with preschoolers.

Telling the Story

When telling a story, there are important things to consider such as:

Elements of Good Storytelling

Some basic characteristics that all storytellers should have include good voice and diction, a complete sincerity and joy in storytelling, and a flair for the dramatic. Storytellers are not actors, but it does help for them to have a sense of the dramatic.

Appeal to the Eye

Body movement is very important. Be natural and at ease. Stand or sit in a relaxed manner. Although it is not necessary to remain stiff while telling a story, do not overdramatize your actions. Nonverbal language conveys as much meaning as verbal language when telling a story. Use natural hand movements. Do not put your hands in pockets or cross your arms in front of you. If nothing else feels natural and comfortable, put your hands behind you. Facial expressions and gestures can add emphasis to a story if they are natural and spontaneous. For example, arm, hand, and facial muscle movements; raised eyebrows; and nose twitches can add emphasis to a particular point or action.

Eye contact with your audience is of prime importance. It is probably the single most important element of good storytelling. Look at all of the children in the group, not just one. Catch the eyes of different children as you relate the story. Keeping your audience captive with good eye contact will make the children feel more involved with the story.

Appeal to the Ear

Clear and distinctive speech is best achieved by practicing the story. Make sure that your voice is loud enough to be heard by the children farthest from you without having to shout. It is important to be seen and heard by every person in the audience. Try to keep your voice from dropping at the ends of sentences. Do not hurry through the story, but keep a slow, steady pace even though at times you may feel that the pace is too slow. Use pauses for emphasis and variety.

Getting a feel for the pace and timing of a story is extremely important. Some stories require a slow and stately pace, (*Snow White*), while others demand a rapid pace (Eric Carle's *The Grouchy Ladybug*). Use pauses and an occasional dropped voice to convey changes in a story. A pause before a new idea can indicate much to the listener. The use of effective pauses is often a device of a good storyteller rather than a nervous and forgetful one. Some parts of a story, especially long descriptive passages, require a slower, gentler pace than action passages do.

When telling a story with dialogue, adapt your tone and pace to fit the character who is speaking. For example, a giant in *Jack and the Beanstalk* would speak in a slow, deep manner while the character Chicken Little would speak in a high-pitched, hurried manner. Adjust your tone to that of the story. If there are rhythmic singsong phrases in the story, then use a singsong tone of voice to convey the essence of the phrases. Although adjusting voice tone and pace to that of a story character is essential, do not overdo it by trying to convey several different characters with your voice. It is best to use only your normal voice at a different pace rather than to try to develop separate characters with distinctive voices. For example, in *The Three Bears*, it is not necessary to create different voices for each of the bears. Formal voice characterizations should be used only by people who have had formal voice training.

One way to control voice pitch and tone is through breath control. Breathing from the upper chest gives the voice a higher pitched quality and a lighter, softer tone. Breathing from the abdomen produces a rich fuller tone of voice, which indicates strength and vitality.

Physical Surroundings

Most storytellers have to "make do" with whatever facilities are available. Story sessions can take place inside or outside depending on the occasion. However, there are some ways to ease problems that may occur.

Seating—If you are using a classroom, students can sit in their seats in rows, but such seating tends to make the storytelling session feel like a mandatory class rather than a pleasurable experience. To make the atmosphere less formal, the students can sit in a semicircle either in chairs or on the floor. The semicircle arrangement works well in libraries. The circle should be small enough for the storyteller to see all the children without constantly turning his or her head. The children should be seated so that each child can see the storyteller as well as be seen.

If a separate room is not available, use screens to create a sense of privacy or to create a special story-time corner in a quiet area of the library. Establish a story corner in an area away from room traffic. A regular area used only for story time gives the children a sense of importance about the storytelling. Try to avoid risers, bleachers, and auditoriums for storytelling sessions because these settings place the storyteller below the level of the audience and thus at a disadvantage.

Lighting—Do not have the audience face sunlight and windows that may distract from the storytelling. The same holds true for traffic patterns in the library. The audience should not face any room traffic in the storytelling area. If special lighting is needed to establish the story atmosphere (such as a darkened room for ghost stories), be sure to arrange for such lighting beforehand.

Heat and ventilation—Check the heat flow and airflow before the story session begins. A room that is too hot or too cold can distract the listeners from the story.

Sitting versus standing—Whether a storyteller sits or stands depends on a number of factors. Sitting is comfortable when talking to small groups and with younger children. It provides a more intimate setting and increases the feeling that the audience will get most of the impact of the story through listening. However, if the children are seated on the floor, it is often better for the storyteller to sit on a small bench or stool slightly above the audience. It is often necessary to be seated if you are using puppets or flannelboard figures as part of the story session.

Many storytellers who use traditional methods believe that standing is the best method for relating tales. Standing provides a more formal atmosphere by separating the teller from the listeners and creating a feeling of the theater. The standing storyteller has better control over the audience, with a better eye span and more freedom of movement. Outdoor locations can be more difficult than indoor ones because acoustics and outdoor noises such as traffic are distracting. When conducting storytelling programs outdoors, try to find a shady, quiet spot away from the mainstream of traffic, children playing, and other distractions.

Things Not to Do

Moralize—Not every story is designed to teach a lesson and even if it is, it is not necessary for the storyteller to use a story as a stepping stone for a lecture.

Interruptions—Keep interruptions and comments to a minimum, especially true if the same child keeps interrupting the story to relate a personal anecdote

or reminiscence that has nothing to do with the story. An occasional comment or question from a child will not disrupt the flow of the story. At times, especially with younger children, asking questions or making comments is a natural part of the story session and helps hold the children's interest. The read-aloud story *On Market Street* by Arnold Lobel is an example of a story in which interruptions are encouraged. When I tell this story, I read the first page of the rhyme in a fast-paced voice. As I show the pictures for the next page, I tell the children what the girl bought that begins with the letter A and then B. For the rest of the book, on every other double-page spread, I ask the children to tell me what they think the girl bought that begins with the next letter of the alphabet.

Don't have the children analyze the story—If the children want to discuss the story at the conclusion of the session, then hold a discussion but do not analyze the action. Too much analysis detracts from the pleasure of a story.

Things to Do

Dress—Although lots of jewelry and bright scarves are eye appealing, they can be distracting to children, so avoid long dangling earrings, clanging bracelets, and the like when telling a story. Dress in bright cheerful attire that does not distract from listening to the story. At times, it is fun and exciting to dress in the costume of a character or a time period in a story. Dressing up as a witch at Halloween or all in red to tell *Little Red Riding Hood* adds spice to the story session.

Positive attitude—Smiles, warmth, and genuine pleasure in the story all convey a message to the audience.

Direction—Direct the story particularly to any restless child in the audience. At times, you can call a restless child by name as you tell the story so that the child's attention is directed back to the story.

Introducing a Story

Keep the introduction to a story or program brief. An introduction helps set the mood of the program. Ways to introduce a story include (1) making a personal comment on the type or style of the story or theme of the program, (2) providing some background information on the author or book (keep it brief), and (3) simply showing the book to the children and stating the title and author. When introducing *On Market Street*, you might begin by commenting on how much fun it is to go shopping for gifts for others and lead into the story by stating that this is the tale of a little girl who goes shopping for a gift.

Many storytellers use props to introduce a story and to set the mood for the program. The props can range from puppets or stuffed storybook characters to inanimate objects such as music boxes, rocks, or figurines—anything that plays a role in the story. A number of companies and bookstores sell models of storybook characters that you might find useful. Max and the Wild Things, Clifford the Big Red Dog, Curious George, Paddington Bear, Corduroy, Ramona, and Rotten Ralph are only a few of the book characters currently available. Puzzles, a treasure trunk, postcards, dolls, blocks, maps, live animals, and toys are other types of items that can be used to introduce a story.

Choosing the Medium

Choosing a medium for story presentation is a personal decision to be made by the storyteller. In addition to traditional storytelling, a number of different mediums can be used including puppets, creative dramatics, read-alouds, pantomime, flannelboards, tandem telling, and singing tales.

Whether props are used to help tell a story depends on the storyteller. Some storytellers believe that using props such as puppets or a flannelboard makes it easier to face an audience and adds another dimension to the story, while others believe that props are just something extra to worry about and distract from the story.

For small audiences (fewer than 15 children), traditional storytelling, read-alouds for picture books, and finger puppets are good choices. For a large audience (15 to 30 children), participation stories, oversized books or tagboard stories, hand puppets without a formal theater, and traditional storytelling work well. For very large audiences (more than 30 children), attention-getting devices such as flannelboards, shadow plays, large puppets on a formal stage, and creative dramatics as well as traditional storytelling help to maintain interest.

There are as many different ways to present a story as there are storytellers. The presentation medium depends on the story, the size and type of audience, time constraints, and the personal preferences of the storyteller.

Story File

Keep a file of each story that you use in a storytelling program. Although this task may seem like a lot of bother, the file is quite useful if you plan to do a lot of storytelling. Such a file can ensure that you do not repeat the same story with the same group of children every year.

Index cards or some kind of storytelling record form works best for keeping your file. For each story that you use, include the author, title, other bibliographic information, type of story, any mediums that you used with the story (puppet, flannelboard, tagboard, etc.), date or dates the story was used, where you used the story (grade level, class name, and children in the group), comments on the failure or success of the program, and other comments on the story session.

Aftermath: Follow-up Activities

In the main text (the discussions of specific stories) of this book, you will find a number of different types of follow-up activities ranging from treats to puzzles and craft activities. Follow-up and related activities for story programs depend on personal preferences, time constraints, and age levels.

Simple mementos or giveaways can be significant reminders of a special story. Although it is not necessary or even important to give children mementos at each story session, the giveaways can be nice enhancements to a special session or program and are a natural extension to the story. Many books lend themselves to providing specific inexpensive or virtually free souvenirs of the story. For example, with *Sylvester and the Magic Pebble* by William Steig or *"There Are Rocks in My Socks!" Said the Ox to the Fox* by Patricia Thomas, give each child a brightly colored rock or aquarium stone to take home. With *The Carrot Seed* by Ruth Kraus, give seeds to take home and plant; with *If You Give a Mouse a Cookie* by Laura Joffe Numeroff, pass out chocolate chip cookies; with *The Great Valentine's Day Balloon Race* by Adrienne Adams, use balloons; and with *Flat Stanley* by Jeff Brown, give balls of clay. Fortune cookies, candles, raisins, pumpkin seeds, popcorn, seashells, nutshells or any number of other objects can be used as mementos of a special story.

A Final Note

If you are conducting formal storytime programs on a regular basis, you will probably develop a pattern to the program. The following is an example of possible steps in a story program:

- Greet the children as they enter.

- Pin name tags on the children.

- As you wait for all of the children to arrive, give the children who have arrived books to look at or let them browse at will.

- Point out special exhibits or displays that may be of interest to the group.

- Use some kind of signal (for example, lighting a candle or using a puppet or storytime mascot) to indicate that stories are about to begin and to signal a time for quiet.

- Start the program on time with a theme song, when children take hands and march into the storytelling area.

- Follow the song with appropriate actions (for example, train movements for a train program).

- Spend a few minutes talking with the group. (For example, discuss what happened during the week or have a sharing time with an object, toy, etc.)

- Use a finger play to bring the group to attention.

- Introduce and tell the first story (which is usually the longest one).

- If anyone in the group has had a birthday during the past week or since you last met, sing "Happy Birthday." You might celebrate once a month for all the children who have birthdays that month.

- Present the second story, a poem, nursery rhymes, dramatizations, etc.

- For longer story programs or special events, use filmstrips, movies, special occasion parties with treats, or a special visitor with a unique tale to enhance the program.

- Close with good-byes, with or without a puppet or story mascot. Have the children return the name tags. At the end of each month, let the children take their name tags home.

- Allow children to select books to take home.

Endnote

1. Dinesen, Isak. "The Cardinal's First Tale," in *Last Tales*. New York: Random House, 1957. p.23.

Traditional Storytelling

The term storytelling brings forth the image of a lively troubadour recounting an exciting adventure. Typically, the audience leans forward with interest and anticipation. In the traditional mode, storytellers are so familiar with the plot, the characters, and the action, that they can relate the tales as if they were a part of their personal family histories.

From the beginnings of mankind, storytelling has been an integral part of human life. Before the printed word, stories were passed from one generation to the next by trained storytellers. Storytellers were the keepers of history and culture. They were often viewed with respect and awe and regarded as individuals with magical powers. During the Middle Ages, troubadours wandered the countryside using music and poetry to spread folktales and legends across Europe. Even with the advent of the printing press and the mass production of printed materials, traditional stories and storytellers continued to play an important role in preserving the folktales and traditions of many ethnic groups and cultures. In the United States, the art of storytelling was kept alive in libraries and in some cultures, but it was not a skill that was actively practiced during much of the twentieth century.

Since the early 1970s, there has been a resurgence of interest in the art of storytelling using both the methods of traditional oral storytelling and some new and innovative techniques. Traditional storytellers use only their voices, expressions, gestures, and the power of the words to relate their tales to listeners. Although experienced storytellers give polished performances, anyone can become a storyteller. Follow some of the techniques and methods mentioned in the introduction and anyone can master the art of storytelling. Although much of the information is general in nature, the methods are ones used first by traditionalists and later applied to other situations. The Internet is filled with Web sites that link to sources for stories, techniques to use, and pages of tips from professional storytellers. In any case, the first rule that anyone should learn is *to have fun!* Storytelling serves many purposes, and among the most important is that of entertaining and enriching the lives of listeners.

The Aminal

by Lorna Balian
Abingdon, 1972

Summary: Patrick finds a pet to take home and has the whole neighborhood believing that he has a wild thing in a paper bag.

Procedure: This delightful story about an information mix-up is good to use for traditional storytelling. However, if you like to use props, there are a number of different ways to enhance the storytelling. One idea that is used by the wonderful puppeteer Connie Champlin is to place a small stuffed turtle in a paper bag. Before presenting the story, bring the bag out, shake it, and ask the children to guess what is in the bag. After a few guesses, tell them that it is an aminal. At this point, begin to tell the story. After you are finished and the identity of the aminal is revealed, open the paper bag and pull out the stuffed turtle.

Another idea is to have a real turtle for the children to see and touch after you have finished the story. If there is time, talk about turtles, what they eat, where they live, etc., or give each child an information sheet on turtles to take home.

A third alternative is to discuss with the audience what other animals Patrick might have found. Fill a small bag with strange plastic "aminals," and let each child choose one to take home.

Optional Activities

Tub Turtles

Cut out a turtle head, legs, and a tail from construction paper. Place the lid from a small margarine tub upside down on a flat surface, and fit the head, legs, and tail on the lid. Place the margarine tub on the lid and snap it shut. Everything will stay in place once the lid is snapped shut. Be sure that the ends of the pieces are long enough to stay inside the margarine tub lid. Adjust the head, legs and tail to the desired angles. When completed, each child will have a turtle to take home.

Materials needed:
- small margarine tubs with lids
- construction paper
- scissors

Mosaic Turtles

Give each child a sheet containing the outline of a turtle. Each child should draw eyes, legs, a tail, and a shell on the picture. The children can cut out small squares of paper and glue them to the picture to create a colorful patterned shell.

Materials needed:
- activity sheet with outline of a turtle
- construction paper
- glue and/or paste
- scissors

Related Books: Puns and Memory Games

Arnold, Tedd. *Ollie Forgot!* New York: Dial, 1988. Ollie's unreliable memory gets him into trouble as he makes his way to the market.

Gwynne, Fred. *A Chocolate Moose for Dinner.* New York: Simon & Schuster, 1976. Each page in this book offers a pun about phrases in the English language, including the cover with a chocolate moose sitting at a table.

Patz, Nancy. *Pumpernickel Tickle and Mean Green Cheese.* New York: Franklin Watts, 1978. To remember the grocery list, Benjamin and Elephant create fantastic food rhymes and puns.

Giveaways

"All About Turtles" fact sheet, and an "aminal" of their own. Fill a grab bag with strange plastic creatures such as those given away at Halloween. Let each child reach into the bag and pick out an "aminal" to take home.

Preparation time
Story: 10–25 min.
Optional Activities
Tub Turtles: 10–25 min.
Mosaic Turtles: 10–20 min.

All About Turtles

Hibernation

Species that live where the winters are harsh will hibernate.
- Fresh water turtles live in warm muddy bottom of ponds and stream waters.
- Land turtles bury themselves in soil or rotting vegetation.

Types of Turtles

- Mud/marsh
- Pond/marsh
- Sea
- Side-necked
- Snapping
- Soft-shelled
- Tortoise

Turtle Facts

- There are over 250 species
- Forty species are endangered because they are hunted for their meat and eggs
- Turtles lay their eggs and let the sun hatch them
- Turtles cannot live in areas that are cold all year
- Most turtle growth takes place in the first fifty years
- Turtles are reptiles with shells
- Pond/marsh turtles are the largest family with over 90 species
- Turtles eat animals and plants
- The largest sea turtle—the leatherback—can grow 4 to 8 feet long

The Cobweb Christmas

By Shirley Climo • Illustrated by Joe Lasker

Crowell, 1982

Summary: After waiting years to witness the magic of Christmas, a kind old woman finally gets her wish.

Procedure: This story is good to use at the beginning of December as an introduction to the Christmas season. It could be used as a kick-off to decorating the library and a tree for the holiday season. There are several key words and key phrases in the story that make it relatively easy to learn for traditional storytelling. While you are telling the story, string a strand of silver stars to hang on a tree or to decorate the room.

Optional Activities

Because this story serves as a good beginning to the holiday season, you can use it to introduce a number of art projects to make decorations for the room and tree.

Tinsel Stars

While you tell the story and string silver stars, have the children make strands of their own. The children can cut out large silver stars and string them for strands of tinsel. You can also use the separate large silver stars by themselves as tree ornaments.

Materials needed:
- silver paper (Mylar or aluminum foil)
- scissors
- string

Popcorn Chains

At one time or another everyone has made a popcorn chain. The children can make single strands of popcorn or mix the popcorn and the silver stars to make tinsel.

Materials needed:
- string
- needles
- scissors
- popped corn (1- or 2-day-old popcorn works better than fresh popcorn)

Paper Chains

This activity is especially good to use with younger children, but all ages will enjoy making paper chains. Use either precut strips of construction paper, or have the children cut their own strips. Fasten the chains together with tape, and hang them on the tree or decorate the room with them.

Materials needed:
- construction paper
- scotch tape
- scissors

Related Books: Christmas Is Coming

Moore, Clement C. *The Night Before Christmas.* Illustrated by Anita Lobel. New York: Knopf, 1984. This is only one of the dozens of editions of the classic poem about Christmas Eve.

Spier, Peter. *Peter Spier's Christmas.* New York: Doubleday, 1983. This is a wordless picture book on the joys of Christmas.

Strickland, Henrietta. *The Christmas Bear.* Illustrated by Paul Strickland. New York: Dutton, 1993. When a curious little polar bear falls through a hole in the snow, he ends up in the magical kingdom of Santa.

Tyler, Linda Wagner. *The After Christmas Tree.* Illustrated by Susan Davis. New York: Viking, 1990. A family decorates their leftover Christmas tree with edible goodies for the animals and birds.

Van Allsburg, Chris. *The Polar Express.* Boston: Houghton Mifflin, 1985. A small boy boards a train bound for the North Pole one Christmas Eve.

 Preparation time
Story: 30–45 min.
Optional Activities
Tinsel Stars: 5–15 min.
Popcorn Chains: 5–15 min.
Paper Chains: 5–15 min.

The Easter Egg Artists

by Adrienne Adams

Scribner, 1976

Summary: The Abbott rabbit family designed and decorated traditional Easter eggs until the day their son, Orson, designs comic eggs and turns the world of decorating upside down.

Procedure: Use this story before Easter, and introduce it as a tale of rabbits, eggs, and decorating.

Optional Activities

Crisscross Eggs

Cut out oval shapes (egg pattern on p. 20) from Styrofoam or white cardboard, and cut slits around the edges. Cut yarn into short lengths (6–10"). Tape one end of a piece of yarn to the back of the egg shape, and pull it through one of the slits. Crisscross the yarn strands across the egg shape to create a design.

Materials needed:

- Styrofoam (weight of retail meat platters) or lightweight white cardboard
- assorted yarns
- scissors
- tape

Comic Designs

Give each child a plastic egg to decorate with a comic face or design. Use, for example, assorted pieces of cloth, cotton, fur, or yarn; sequins; or buttons to create the designs.

Materials needed:

- plastic eggs
- scraps of cotton, yarn, fur, or cloth
- sequins
- buttons
- other materials for decoration

Related Books: Easter Eggs

Armour, Richard. *The Adventures of Egbert the Easter Egg.* Pictures by Paul Galdone. New York: McGraw-Hill, 1965. Egbert gets a very special face and a host of adventures one special Easter.

Auch, Mary Jane. *The Easter Egg Farm.* New York: Holiday House, 1992. When Pauline lays eggs in all sorts of colors, patterns, and designs, she becomes the talk of the town.

Kroll, Steven. *The Big Bunny and the Easter Egg.* Illustrated by Janet Stevens. New York: Holiday House, 1982. Who will do Wilbur the Easter bunny's job when he gets sick?

Kunhardt, Edith. *Danny and the Easter Egg.* New York: Greenwillow, 1989. Danny and his friends color Easter eggs and go on an egg hunt.

Stevenson, James. *The Great Big Especially Beautiful Easter Egg.* New York: Greenwillow, 1983. Grandpa sets out to find a very large Easter egg.

Giveaways

Easter eggs

⏰	**Preparation time**
	Story: 5–15 min.
	Optional Activities
	Crisscross Eggs 5–15 min.
	Comic Designs 5–15 min.

Crisscross Eggs

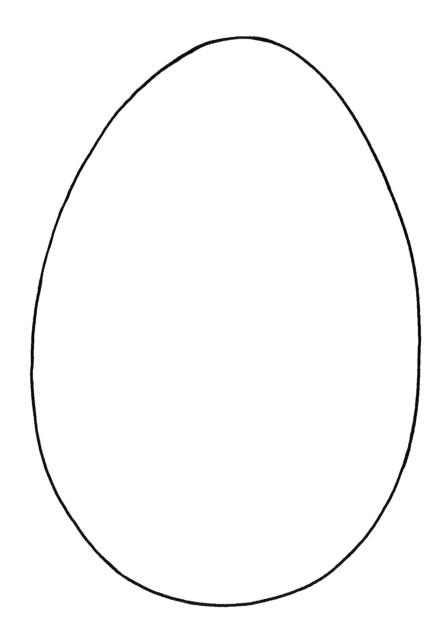

Everyone Knows What a Dragon Looks Like

By Jay Williams • Illustrated by Mercer Mayer

Four Winds, 1976

Summary: A small road sweeper's strong belief in and common courtesy to a dragon are responsible for the dragon saving the city of Wu from the Wild Horseman of the North.

Procedure: Like many folktales, this story is especially suited for traditional storytelling. First, read the story for pure enjoyment. Then, read it to learn the basic sequence of events, to absorb the flavor of the language, and to identify the main characters. Learn the story using the methods that work best for you. The pictures in the book are beautiful, but it is best not to show them to the children and thus to encourage each child to create his or her own image of a dragon.

Optional Activities

While explaining each activity, use the phrase "Everyone knows what a dragon looks like" several times.

Dragon Drawings

Give the children sheets of paper, and explain that they are to draw pictures of what they think a dragon looks like. Display the drawings on a bulletin board in the library. You can use the drawings in connection with a display of books and other materials about dragons and monsters.

Materials needed:
- pencils or crayons
- paper

Dragon Mural

Instead of the children doing individual drawings, they can create a group mural. Have the children describe what they think a dragon looks like. Make a list of the features that they name (for example, a large head and a long nose). You can use the list in one of two ways. (1) You can draw a dragon the way

the children perceive it by using their descriptions (the same way a police artist creates a sketch), or (2) the children can create a group mural showing the dragon the way they perceive it to look.

Materials needed:
- large piece of white paper
- markers, pencils, or crayons

Related Books: Of Knights and Dragons

dePaola, Tomie. *The Knight and the Dragon.* New York: Viking, 1980. This almost wordless book is about a fierce battle between an inexperienced knight and a very young dragon.

Hodges, Margaret. *Saint George and the Dragon.* Boston: Little, Brown, 1984. This is a retelling from Spenser's *The Faerie Queen,* where George the Red Cross Knight slays the dragon that has been terrorizing the countryside.

Kent, Jack. *The Once-Upon-A-Time Dragon.* New York: Harcourt Brace Jovanovich, 1982. Sam the dragon longs to be a man.

Prelutsky, Jack. *The Dragons Are Singing Tonight.* Pictures by Peter Sis. New York: Greenwillow, 1993. This remarkable collection of dragon poems will delight and terrify readers.

Wilson, Sarah. *Beware the Dragons!* New York: Harper and Row, 1985. A little girl sails across the bay and finds some dragons who want to play.

Preparation time

Story: 1–2 hours

Optional Activities

    Dragon Wings: 5–20 min.

    Mosaic Turtles: 5–20 min.

The Five Chinese Brothers

by Clarie Huchet Bishop and Kurt Wiese
Coward-McCann, 1938

Summary: In this modern day classic, five brothers, each with a special talent, escape the wrath of the villagers and live happily by the sea.

Procedure: This folktale is very easy to learn and especially good for traditional storytelling. The repetitive phrases are quickly learned and make the story a lot of fun for the storyteller and the listeners.

Optional Activities

A Special Talent
Give each child a sheet of paper and have them draw one of the brothers from the story or a new brother. As the child draws the brother, incorporate a special talent into the drawing. Then write a brief description of the brother and the special talent that he has.

> *Materials needed:*
> • pencils, markers, or crayons
> • paper

Related Books: How Clever We Are

Mahy, Margaret. *The Seven Chinese Brothers.* Illustrated by Jean and Mousien Tseng. New York: Scholastic, 1990. Seven brothers use their special powers to outsmart the Emperor.

Numeroff, Laura. *The Chicken Sisters.* Illustrated by Sharleen Collicott. New York: HarperCollins, 1997. When a big bad wolf moves to town, he thinks the chicken sisters will be easy prey, only to have the threesome knit, bake, and sing him to distraction.

Patron, Susan. *Burgoo Stew.* Illustrated by Mike Shenon. New York: Orchard, 1991. Five hungry, rowdy boys demand some burgoo stew from Billy Que, an old man who enlists their aid to create the special treat.

Stevens, Janet. *Tops and Bottoms.* San Diego: Harcourt, 1995. The clever rabbit convinces the lazy bear to share his garden bounty.

Preparation time
Story: 15–30 min.
Optional Activities
  A Special Talent: 15–20 min.

The Pumpkin Smasher

by Anita Bernarde

Walker, 1972

Summary: When the people of Cranbury awake to discover all their pumpkins destroyed, they are determined to find the pumpkin smasher.

Procedure: Begin the session by holding up a jack-o'-lantern and talking about pumpkins and jack-o'-lanterns as traditional symbols of Halloween. Lead into the story by saying that once in the town of Cranbury, pumpkins almost became extinct.

Optional Activities

Pumpkin Puzzles

Give each child a sheet of orange construction paper. Draw a large jack-o'-lantern on the paper, and divide it into puzzle pieces. Glue the pumpkin to a piece of lightweight cardboard and cut it apart. Place the pieces of each puzzle into a separate envelope for the "puzzlemaker" to take home.

Materials needed:

- orange construction paper
- scissors
- glue
- lightweight cardboard
- markers and/or crayons
- envelopes

Trick-or-Treat Minibags

Cut two pumpkin shapes from orange felt. Using pieces of felt, decorate one of the pumpkin shapes to resemble a jack-o'-lantern. With wrong sides facing, glue the two pumpkin shapes together around the edges leaving the top open. Cut a piece of green ribbon approximately 3"– 4" long. Attach the ribbon on each side of the pumpkin head opening.

Materials needed:

- orange and black felt
- green ribbon
- scissors
- glue

Related Books: Who's Got a Pumpkin?

Cole, Bruce. *The Pumpkinville Mystery.* Englewood Cliffs, NJ: Prentice-Hall, 1987. A mysterious stranger is responsible for good triumphing over evil on one Halloween night.

Cuyler, Marilyn. *Sir William and the Pumpkin Man.* Illustrated by Marsha Winborn. New York: Holt, Rinehart, and Winston, 1984. When a ghost is unsuccessful in scaring the family in his old house, he finds himself the one who's frightened.

Kellogg, Steven. *The Mystery of the Flying Orange Pumpkin.* New York: Dial, 1980. When Mr. Klug moves in next door, he decides to make a pumpkin pie out of the pumpkin that Brian, Ellis, and Joan intended to use as a giant jack-o'-lantern.

Stevenson, James. *That Terrible Halloween Night.* New York: Greenwillow, 1980. Grandpa tells Mary Ann and Louis all about a ghostly old house where all sorts of mysterious things happen.

White, Linda. *Too Many Pumpkins.* Illustrated by Megan Floyd. New York: Holiday House, 1996. Estelle hates pumpkins, but somehow she finds herself with a yard full of them.

Giveaway

Cookies decorated to look like jack-o'-lanterns

 Preparation time
Story: 30–45 min.
Optional Activities
 Pumpkin Puzzles: 15–20 min.
 Trick-or-Treat Minibags: 10–20 min.

Socks for Supper

by Jack Kent

Parents' Magazine Press, 1978

Summary: When a poor couple exchange socks for milk and cheese, they receive an unexpected gift.

Procedure: Begin the session by stating that the story is about a very poor couple who receive an unexpected gift. Because the story is relatively short, it is a good tale to use on days when you do not have much time or when you need another story to fill in the last few minutes of a class.

Optional Activities

Lacy Stockings
Cut out two sock shapes from construction paper. Punch a series of holes around the outside edges of the two shapes. Use shoe laces or yarn, and lace the two sock shapes.

> *Materials needed:*
> - construction paper
> - scissors
> - hole puncher
> - shoe laces or yarn

Sock Puppets
This activity is best suited for older children (in grades 2 to 4). Give each child a sock to use as the base for the puppet. Demonstrate to the children how to give the puppet a personality by adding facial features and making the puppet appear to talk. Let the children decorate their puppets with an assortment of craft materials.

> *Materials needed:*
> - old socks
> - scissors
> - scraps of fabric, felt, lace, and yarn
> - assorted buttons
> - glue

Socks for Everyone (activity sheet)
Give each child an activity sheet with an outline of a sock on it. The children are to draw more socks and designs for socks.

Related Books: Socks

Balian, Lorna. *The Socksnatchers.* Nashville: Abingdon, 1988. The Perkins family never suspects that there are socksnatchers, who are responsible for all the missing socks, living in their cellar.

Murphy, Stuart J. *A Pair of Socks.* Illustrated by Lois Elbert. New York: HarperCollins, 1996. A sock searches the house for its mate.

Selden, George. *Sparrow Socks.* Illustrated by Peter Lippman. New York: Harper, 1965. Angus makes small socks for sparrows and ensures that everyone has a pair.

Thomas, Patricia. *"There Are Rocks in My Socks!" Said the Ox to the Fox.* Illustrated by Mordicai Gerstein. New York: Lothrop, Lee & Shepard, 1979. The ox asks all his friends for advice on getting rid of the rocks in his socks.

Giveaway
"Socks for Everyone" (activity sheet)

	Preparation time
	Story: 5–10 min.
	Optional Activities
	Lazy Stockings: 5–15 min.
	Sock Puppets: 10–25 min.
	Socks for Everyone: 5–15 min.

Socks for Everyone

What kind of socks do you like? Draw more socks and designs that the old man and woman might trade for food.

The Whingdingdilly

by Bill Peet
Houghton Mifflin, 1970

Summary: When Scamp meets a witch who turns him into a whingdingdilly, he discovers that being a plain old dog is okay after all.

Procedure: Introduce the story by talking about make-believe animals and how they can look any way you want them to look. Tell the group the title of the story, and explain that you want them to listen very carefully to the description of this strange creature. When the story is over, ask each child to draw a picture of the whingdingdilly. The pictures should be placed on display for everyone to see. **Do not** show any of the book illustrations to the group.

Optional Activities

What's a Whingdingdilly?

Give each child a piece of drawing paper and a pencil. As you read the story, have each child create a picture of his or her image of the whingdingdilly in the story. After the children share their pictures with the group, show the book illustrations and see how they compare with the children's images.

Materials needed:
- drawing paper
- pencils
- crayons and/or markers

Make Your Own Whingdingdilly

Give each child a piece of modeling clay, and ask each to create his or her own whingdingdilly.

Materials needed:
- modeling clay
- old newspapers

Related Books: Strange Critters

Brandenberg, Franz. *Otto Is Different.* New York: Greenwillow, 1985. Otto discovers that having eight arms can have its advantages.

Brown, Marc. *Arthur's Nose.* Boston: Little, Brown, 1976. Arthur, the aardvark, goes to the doctor to try to find a new nose.

Kasza, Keiko. *The Pig's Picnic.* New York: Putnam, 1988. Mr. Pig allows his friends to persuade him to change his appearance with some very strange results.

McPhail, David. *The Glerp.* Parseppauy, NJ: Silver Press, 1995. The glerp goes for a walk and eats everything in his way.

Waber, Bernard. *You Look Ridiculous Said the Rhinoceros to the Hippopotamus.* Boston: Houghton Mifflin, 1966. When Hippopotamus tries on other animal parts, she decides that her old self is the best after all.

Preparation time
Story: 10–20 min.
Optional Activities
  What's a Whingdingdilly?: 5–15 min.
  Make Your Own Whingdingdilly:
    5–15 min.

Flannelboard Stories

Flannelboards are a very popular storytelling medium. They are an inexpensive and creative way visually to share stories and to still retain the intimacy and spontaneity of traditional storytelling. A flannelboard is a large stiff board covered with felt, flannel, or some other kind of rough material. As the storyteller speaks, figures are placed on and taken off of the board as visual aids to the story. It is important to choose flannelboard stories with care because the figures take time to prepare. The types of flannelboards include wall, desk, tabletop, and easel styles.

Advantages of Flannelboard Presentations

Flannelboards have the following advantages for both the audience and the storyteller:

- Flannelboard storytelling can stimulate interest, enliven children's imaginations, and encourage an interest in oral language.
- Flannelboards can be arranged, rearranged, and stored easily.
- Flannelboards and figures are easy to make and inexpensive to buy.
- Stories that have long and complex plots or complicated illustrations can be adapted or simplified for use with different age levels.
- Flannelboard stories and figures are flexible and easy to use. The figures can be manipulated by anyone and offer freedom and variety in storytelling programming.
- The figures attract and hold the attention of children because of the movement of the figures onto and off of the flannelboard.
- The figures help bridge the gap between real and abstract concepts because they can be touched, seen, and moved.
- Flannelboard stories are useful in improving communication and in permitting children to participate in the storytelling process.

- Flannelboard storytelling allows the storyteller to use elements and concepts appropriate for the age level of the audience.

Choosing a Story

For use with the flannelboard, it is best to select a story with a simple plot and only a few characters. However, if you choose to tell a more complex story, you can adapt the illustrations and plot action for flannelboard use. Cumulative tales and rhymes work very well as do folktales and many picturebook stories. By using only a few figures, the storyteller can pay attention to the plot and the audience rather than devote most of his or her time to adding and removing felt characters.

The Flannelboard

A flannelboard may be purchased from any school supply store or it can be homemade. Purchased flannelboards range in price from $25 to $75 depending on the size and type. They range in size from 18"x 24" to 36"x 48" and are available in folding sizes.

When making your own flannelboard, use a material that is stiff enough not to bend or to sag, but yet is lightweight enough to carry easily from place to place. To make a permanent flannelboard, use a 24"x 36" piece of plywood or composition board and thumbtack, tape, or staple the felt or flannel to the board. Pull the fabric tight so that you have a smooth surface. Do not glue the material to the board. Glue lessens the static electricity that causes the figures to adhere to the board. If you have trouble with figures staying on the board, rub the board with a cloth to charge the static electricity field so the figures will stay in place. Felt thumbtacked to a piece of plywood is the most durable combination. Use a neutral color such as black, dark blue, light blue, or gray for the background. White will also work; however, it gets dirty quickly.

A small cork bulletin board can also double as a

flannelboard. Thumbtack the felt inside the frame of the bulletin board. The cork board has several advantages for the mobile storyteller. The frame can have a handle screwed into it to provide a lightweight carrying board. The felt background can easily be changed to fit the story. For detailed instructions on making different types of flannelboards consult *Trash to Treasures* by Ann Christensen and Lee Green.

If you do not use the flannelboard frequently, cover it with plastic, and store it. Dry cleaning plastic or garbage bags keep dust off of the surface of the board.

Using an easel might be wise. Leaning the board against the back of a chair does not work well; the board can slip and come crashing down in the middle of the story. You can make your own easel or purchase one from a school supply house. Collapsible easels are especially useful to storytellers who move from place to place.

Flannelboard Figures

Flannelboard figures can come from a variety of sources including picture books (especially those with illustrations too small to use with a group), patterns from craft books, or even children's coloring books. If the original pictures are too small, you can enlarge them on a copier. If you do not have access to a copier, draw or trace the figures or use an opaque or overhead projector to enlarge the characters to the desired size.

An easy way to make attractive, useful figures is to copy the characters from the book, color and laminate them, and glue several small felt pieces on the backs of them. The best adhesive to use is hot glue from a glue gun that spreads evenly and dries quickly.

You can use a computer to create flannelboard figures. With the increased availability of scanners and color printers, it is very easy to scan and print illustrations from books to use with flannelboard stories. You can also purchase clip art CD–ROMs that provide a wide array of pictures that can be used on flannelboard. After printing the image, laminate it and place felt on the back. One caution: be aware of the copyright laws regarding fair use and the reproduction of materials for instructional use. If you have any doubts, write or call the publisher and request written permission. You should also attribute the source of the art.

Flannelboard figures can be created using a variety of materials. However, for the best results, use felt or felt-backed figures. Felt adheres to the surface of the board, and the figures are unlikely to fall off during the storytelling session. When using felt, the first step is to cut out the base silhouette of the character or figure. Details can be added by using felt-tipped markers or by gluing small pieces of felt to the base. Felt works best with figures that do not require many details. Tacky glue will work well because it dries clear and spreads evenly.

For figures requiring more details, use lightweight cardboard or plain paper. Trace the figures, cut them out, and color them with crayons or markers. Glue scraps of felt or coarse sandpaper to the back of the figures so that they will adhere to the surface of the flannelboard. Dryer foam sheets can be used as substitutes for felt or sandpaper. From any school supply or craft store, you can purchase rolls of Velcro felt tape to use on the figures.

Nonwoven interfacing is another easy material to use in making figures, and it is readily available from fabric stores. Trace a pattern on the interfacing, cut it out, and color the smooth side with crayons or markers. The rough side will adhere to the flannelboard. Interfacing will not stick to itself, so it cannot be used for figures that overlap.

Other materials that can be used to create flannelboard figures include corduroy, cellophane, suede, monk's cloth, rough rope, blanket fabric, cotton, burlap, sandpaper, blotters, velvet, steel wool, sponges, and all kinds of rough paper. Decorate and enhance the felt figures as well as other materials to add to the board to create a three-dimensional effect. Plastic wiggle eyes can add life to felt people and animals and are available in 3- to 30-millimeter sizes. Polyester fiberfill and pom-poms can be used to create clouds, beards, noses, and animal tails. Pipe cleaners and yarn can be used to make fences, webs, and other decorative items. Feathers, fake fur, glitter, sequins, and beads can add interest and sparkle to the characters. Plastic wrap and cellophane can be used to give the illusion of windows to houses and vehicles.

For the story *The Very Busy Spider* by Eric Carle, you can use yarn to create the web the spider weaves throughout the story. At Halloween, many craft and fabric stores carry decorative spider webs that could be used with this story. The spider webs are inexpensive and add an interesting note to the story.

Practice for a flannelboard story just as you would practice for a traditional storytelling session. Practice placing the figures on and removing them from the board. Have a copy of the story text, and make notations about the movement of felt figures onto and off of the board.

Just before the story session, position the felt characters in the order in which they appear in the story. The storyteller can wear an apron, and store the flannelboard figures in the pockets. (The pockets need to be large enough to prevent the figures from falling out.) This will allow the storyteller the freedom to move around while using the flannelboard. Using a storyteller's apron can increase the children's focus on the story and make it more delightful for them.

Other Presentation Boards

Although flannel or felt boards are the most commonly used boards, storytellers can use other types of presentation boards.

Velcro or Hook 'n' Loop boards are versatile and useful for displaying three-dimensional objects.

Hook 'n' Loop materials are available from school supply or fabric and craft stores; the materials are held in place by many tiny nylon hooks. Velcro provides the same effect as the Hook 'n' Loop except at much lower cost. Rolls and strips of Velcro can be purchased at fabric stores or department stores. One part of the Velcro is attached to the board while the other part is glued to the back of the felt figures.

Magnetic boards are another type of inexpensive display board. You can purchase magnetic boards commercially, or you can create your own using any metal surface (filing cabinet, cookie sheet, scrap metal, etc.). Attach small magnets or a magnetic strip to the back of the display figure to use with stories. You can find the magnetic strips in craft, hardware, and fabric stores. The strips can be cut to any size, and they have adhesive on one side that will stick to fabric, tagboard, or paper.

Any type of presentation board can be used to enhance and to enliven a storytelling program. The boards are relatively inexpensive to make or to buy and provide an imaginative way to share a story visually with children.

Arthur's Nose

by Marc Brown

Little, Brown, 1976

Summary: When Arthur, the aardvark, goes to the doctor to get a new nose, he discovers that changes aren't always for the best.

Procedure: Introduce the story by telling the children that this is one book in a series about Arthur, the aardvark. As you tell the story, place the appropriate felt figures on the flannelboard.

After you finish telling the story, let the children try the different felt noses on Arthur.

An alternative method for presenting this story is the participation method, in which you would use either handmade cardboard noses or purchased ones. Choose a child from the group to play the part of Arthur. As you reach the point in the story where Arthur is trying on pictures of noses, try the noses on the child who is Arthur. Ask the children for their reactions to the noses as Arthur tries each one on.

Materials needed:
- assorted pieces of felt
- black marker to add detail to figures
- scissors

For the story you will need the following characters and items: (1) a house, (2) Arthur's father, (3) Arthur's mother, (4) Arthur's sister, (5) Arthur, (6) Arthur's friend Francine, (7) Doctor Louise, (8) Arthur minus his nose, (9) a series of felt noses including ones for a chicken, fish, elephant, koala bear, hippopotamus, armadillo, toucan, goat, rabbit, mouse, zebra, alligator, and rhinoceros.

Optional Activities

Noses Know

As a follow-up activity have the children change their own appearances by trying on different noses. Make a series of cardboard noses in various sizes and shapes, both animal and human, for the children to try on. Make sure that you have several mirrors available for this activity. As a child tries on a new nose, have the other children try to guess what animal the nose belongs to.

Near Halloween many craft and discount stores sell plastic noses that could also be used with this activity. They are relatively inexpensive depending on the quality and style of the materials.

As a variation on this activity, you can have a bulletin board nearby with the heading, "Changing Noses on Arthur and His Friends." The bulletin board can contain sketches of Arthur and some of his classmates minus their noses. The children can create new noses to try on the book characters.

Materials needed:
- lightweight cardboard
- paint, markers, and crayons
- scissors
- mirrors

Aardvark Puppets

Give each child a paper plate and cardboard tube or craft stick. Tape or glue the stick to the back of the paper plate. Have the children draw eyes and mouths on the faces of the plates but no noses. Make different sizes and shapes of noses from construction paper to attach to the puppet. The children can make only one nose or several noses to take home for their aardvark puppets.

Materials needed:
- paper plates
- cardboard tubes or craft sticks
- construction paper
- masking tape or glue
- coloring medium

Preparation time

Story and figures: 15–20 min.

Optional Activities

Noses Know: 10–20 min.

Aardvark Puppets: 15–25 min.

Give Arthur a New Nose: 5–10 min.

Give Arthur a New Nose
Create an activity sheet with an outline of Arthur's face minus his nose for each child to take home. Each child can give Arthur a new nose and enhance his features as he or she sees fit.

Related Books: All About Noses

Bentley, Nancy. *I've Got Your Nose.* Illustrated by Don Madden. New York: Doubleday, 1991. Unhappy with her tiny button nose, a witch tries to cast a spell to get a new one.

Caple, Kathy. *The Biggest Nose.* Boston: Houghton Mifflin, 1985. Eleanor is very self-conscious about her nose.

Perkens, Se. *The Nose Book.* Illustrated by Roy McKee. New York: Random House, 1970. Noses are very important and serve a vital role, especially for holding up glasses.

Sonnenschein, Harriet. *Harold's Runaway Nose.* New York: Simon & Schuster, 1989. Harold chases his running nose all around the town.

Zalben, Jane Breskin. *A Perfect Nose for Ralph.* Illustrated by John Wallner. New York: Philomel, 1980. When Ralph, the stuffed panda, loses his nose, Reggie tries to find a new one for him.

Giveaway
"Give Arthur a New Nose" (activity sheet)

The Biggest Pumpkin Ever

By Steven Kroll • Illustrated by Jeni Bassett
Holiday House, 1984

Summary: Unaware of each other, Clayton Mouse and Desmond Mouse are raising the same pumpkin, each with very different plans for it.

Procedure: Introduce the story by asking the children what kinds of things are harvested in the fall. Lead into the story by saying that pumpkins are a part of the fall harvest and that the story is about pumpkins and mice. As you tell the story, place the flannelboard figures on the board as they occur in the story.

After the story, briefly discuss pumpkins and how they grow. Take four large index cards or 8½"x11" tagboard and draw illustrations of the four stages of growth for a pumpkin. The stages are a seed, a flowering vine, a green pumpkin, and a ripe pumpkin.

Materials needed:
- assorted felt squares
- black markers
- scissors

The following figures and objects are needed for the story:
- 1 tiny green pumpkin
- 3 progressively larger green pumpkins
- gray city mouse
- brown country mouse
- a house
- 4 decorated blankets
- a blue ribbon
- nose, eyes, and mouth for jack-o'-lantern
- 2 very large pumpkins—1 green and 1 orange face

Optional Activities

This story would be useful to present at the beginning of October. Any of the following activities could be used as decorations in and around the library or classroom.

Pumpkins

Give each child a brown paper lunch bag in which to stuff newspapers. Secure the top of the bag with a twist tie, staple, tape, or rubber band. Paint the bottoms of the bags orange, and decorate them with jack-o'-lantern faces. When all the pumpkins are dry, string them together with green yarn to resemble a pumpkin patch. You could use the string of pumpkins as part of a display on Halloween with witches and other fall items.

Materials needed:
- brown lunch bags
- newspapers
- orange and brown paint
- twist ties, rubber bands, or tape
- green yarn

Clay Jack-o'-Lantern Faces

This activity would be best used with two- to six-year-olds. Give each child a plastic lid and some clay. Dye the clay orange by mixing drops of red and yellow food coloring into the clay. The children press the clay into the plastic lids and decorate it with seeds, buttons, and other items to make jack-o'-lantern faces.

Materials needed:
- clay
- yellow and red food coloring
- plastic lids
- seeds, buttons, and other miscellaneous items for decoration

 Preparation time
Story and figures: 1–2 hours
Optional Activities
  Pumpkins: 10–25 min.
  Clay Jack-o'-Lantern Faces: 5–20 min.
  Paper Jack-o'-Lantern Faces: 5–10 min.
  Carving Pumpkin Faces: 10–30 min.

Paper Jack-o'-Lantern Faces

For young children, cut out round pumpkins shapes from orange construction paper. Let older children cut out the shapes themselves. The children can draw faces on the pumpkins, and the faces can be put up on a bulletin board.

Materials needed:

- orange construction paper
- crayons, markers, and/or paint
- scissors

Carving Pumpkin Faces

After reading the story, carve a jack-o'-lantern from a real pumpkin. Remove the insides prior to the story time.

Materials needed:

- pumpkin
- knife
- newspapers

Related Books: More About Pumpkins

Barth, Edna. *Jack-o'-Lantern*. New York: Clarion, 1974. A nonfiction book relating facts and fallacies about pumpkins, Halloween, and jack-o'-lanterns.

Johnston, Tony. *The Vanishing Pumpkin*. Illustrated by Tomie dePaola. New York: Putnam, 1983. One Halloween, an old man and an old woman set out to find their missing pumpkin.

Fitherington, Jeanne. *Pumpkin Pumpkin*. New York: Greenwillow, 1986. A small boy plants a pumpkin seed and watches as it grows and changes.

Rose, Emma. *Pumpkin Faces*. Illustrated by Judith Moffatt. New York: Scholastic, 1997. Jack-o'-lanterns with all sorts of faces glow on the pages of this small book.

For more pumpkin stories, see the entry for The Pumpkin Smasher *(page 23) in the Traditional Storytelling section.*

Giveaway

Information sheet (with pumpkin seeds attached) showing the four stages of growth for a pumpkin.

Growth Cycle of a Pumpkin

1. Seeds

2. Flowering Vine

3. Green Pumpkin

4. Ripe Pumpkin

Bill and Pete

by Tomie dePaola

Putnam, 1978

Summary: When Bill the Crocodile's captors plan to turn him into a suitcase, Pete, his toothbrush, is the only one who can save him.

Procedure: Introduce the story by placing the two main characters on the flannelboard and giving the title and author of the story. As you read or tell the story, place the appropriate figures on the board.

Materials needed:
- assorted scraps of felt
- felt-tipped markers
- copier
- glue

Flannelboard figures and props needed include (1) a small figure of Bill the Crocodile, (2) Pete the Bird Toothbrush, (3) Bad Guy, (4) several small crocodiles for the school scene, (5) Mother Crocodile, (6) the teacher, Ms. Ibis, (7) a larger figure of Bill the Crocodile, (8) a house, (9) a blackboard, (10) a sign with ABCs on it, (11) signs with names on them, (12) a sign with "Bill" written on it, (13) a river and a riverbank, (14) a cage to place over Bill, (15) a bathtub, and (16) a table with food on it.

To make the flannelboard figures, use a copier to duplicate the illustrations from the book, color in the details, and attach felt to the back of the figures.

Optional Activity

Croc' Pin

Paint a wooden snap-type clothespin and let it dry. Paint eyes and a nose on one end of the clothespin and a design on the back. After the paint dries, cover the clothespin with clear nail polish or with acrylic spray for a shiny finish.

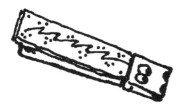

Materials needed:
- wooden snap-type clothespin
- paint
- paintbrush
- clear nail polish or acrylic spray

Related Books: Crocodiles

Aliki. *Keep Your Mouth Closed, Dear.* New York: Dial, 1966. Charles keeps swallowing unwanted items in this hilarious tale.

dePaola, Tomie. *Bill and Pete Go Down the Nile.* New York: Putnam, 1987. On a class trip down the Nile, Bill and Pete encounter a jewelry thief determined to steal the Sacred Eye of Isis.

Duvoisin, Roger. *The Crocodile in the Tree.* New York: Knopf, 1973. A crocodile hides in a tree until he makes friends with Bertha the Duck.

Galdone, Paul. *The Monkey and the Crocodile.* New York: Seabury, 1969. The crocodile tries to trick the monkey.

Waber, Bernard. *Lyle Lyle the Crocodile.* Boston: Houghton Mifflin, 1965. This book is the first in a series of stories about Lyle the Crocodile. It deals with life in the big city for a crocodile.

West, Colin. *Have You Seen the Crocodile?* New York: J. B. Lippincott, 1986. This book is a cumulative tale about the search for the crocodile.

Giveaway

Fact sheet on crocodiles

Preparation time
Story and figures: 1–3 hours
Optional Activities
Croc' Pin: 5–30 min.

Crocodiles

- Are the largest living reptiles—up to 12 feet in length
- Lay their eggs concealed in nests of rubbish and vegetation or buried on sandy beaches
- Have webbed feet that let them walk on land
- Have eyes and nostrils that are higher than the rest of their head
- Have a long, low body
- Have very short legs
- Have sharp teeth and strong jaws that are capable of snapping a boulder in two

Where Can You Find Crocodiles?

They prefer large bodies of shallow water, sluggish rivers, open swamps, and marshes.

Four species are found in North, South and Central America; in the southern tip of Florida, and on the large islands of the West Indies.

Several species of crocodiles are now on the endangered list.

Why?

Because they are hunted for their skin which is used in making shoes and handbags.

Caps for Sale

by Esphyr Slobodkina
Addison Wesley, 1940, 1968

Summary: This timeless tale of a peddler, his caps for sale, and some very strange monkey business still delights children of all ages.

Procedure: The story has an easy-to-follow, free-flowing plot, making it perfect for traditional storytelling accompanied by flannelboard figures. As you tell the story, place the appropriate figures on the board.

Materials needed:
- felt (assorted colors)
- black felt-tipped marker

To make the flannelboard figures, use an opaque projector to enlarge the figures from the book for transfer to felt. You will need the following figures: (1) the peddler, (2) caps (four each of gray, brown, blue, and red), (3) a large sun smiling down on the peddler, (4) a tree with several branches, (5) sixteen monkeys to wear the caps, (6) and one plaid cap to match the peddler's pants.

Optional Activities

Trying One on for Size
After telling the story, bring out a box full of different kinds of hats. Let children try on hats and look in mirrors to see how they look. Be sure to have several styles, colors, and types of hats available, including berets, pillboxes, cowboy hats, scarves, and derbies.

Materials needed:
- hats of all kinds, shapes, and colors
- mirrors

What Kind of Hats Do You Like? (activity sheet)
This activity sheet is good to use in conjunction with "Trying One on for Size." Each child can draw a picture of herself and friends trying on different hats.

Make Your Own Hat (activity sheet)
Making newspaper hats to take home is a good way to help the children remember the story time. Take a sheet of newspaper and fold it as shown in the directions on the activity sheet. You may wish to write each child's name on his or her hat to avoid confusion.

Materials needed:
- old newspapers
- wide black felt-tipped marker

Related Books: Hats and More Hats

Brett, Jan. *The Hat.* New Yok: Putnam, 1997. When Hedgie tries on a stocking and pretends it is a new hat, all his friends laugh at him.

Johnston, Tony. *The Witch's Hat.* Illustrated by Margot Tomes. New York: Putnam, 1984. When a witch's hat falls into the magic pot, she has a terrible time trying to retrieve it as it changes form.

Keats, Ezra Jack. *Jennie's Hat.* New York: Harper and Row, 1966. Disappointed at the plain hat that her aunt gives her, Jennie does her best to decorate it.

Nodset, Joan L. *Who Took the Farmer's Hat?* Illustrated by Fritz Siebel. New York: Harper and Row, 1963. A farmer looks everywhere for his missing hat.

Seuss, Dr. *The 500 Hats of Bartholomew Cubbins.* New York: Vanguard, 1938. Every time Bartholomew removes his hat for the king, another one appears on his head.

Smith, William Jay. *Ho for a Hat.* Boston: Joy Street, 1989. All kinds of hats are celebrated in this tale of a boy and his dog.

Van deer Meer, Ron and Atie. *Funny Hats.* New York: Random House, 1992. Lift the hat-shaped flaps and count the funny hats worn by the animals.

Giveaway
Directions for "Make Your Own Hat"

 Preparation time
Story and figures: 30–40 min.
Optional Activities
Trying One on for Size: 10–20 min.
What Kind of Hats Do You Like? 10–20 min.
Make Your Own Hat: 10–30 min.

What Kind of Hats Do You Like?

Draw pictures of you and your friends and the hats that you like to wear.

Make Your Own Hat

Take a sheet of newspaper and fold it in the direction indicated below. When you are finished, write your name across the side of the hat.

1.  FOLD

2. 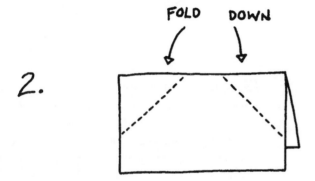 FOLD DOWN

3. 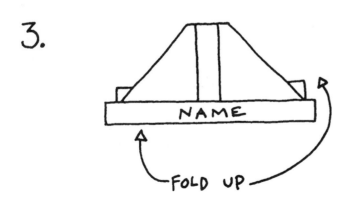 NAME — FOLD UP

The Fat Cat
A Danish Folktale

by Jack Kent
Parents Magazine Press, 1971

Summary: In this cumulative folktale, a cat eats everything in sight until he meets up with a woodcutter and his axe.

Procedure: Introduce the story by asking if anyone has a pet cat. Ask what it eats. Spend a few minutes discussing what a cat usually eats, and then tell the children you have a story about a fat cat who eats some very strange things. As you tell the story, add and remove the flannelboard characters from the board. As the cat continues his eating spree, make the felt cat become larger and larger so that he covers about half of the board by the time he meets the woodcutter. For the final lines of the story, remove the fat cat from the flannelboard, put up all the characters in reverse order, and finally add the cat with a bandage on his stomach.

Materials needed:
- felt
- rubber cement or hot glue and glue gun
- felt-tipped markers
- scissors
- laminating materials
  (contact paper will work)

Make freehand copies of the illustrations from the actual book. Color the figures with felt-tipped markers, and attach felt to the back of the characters before you cut them out. You will need the following characters: (1) an old woman, (2) the pot holding the gruel, (3) Skohenttentot, (4) Skolinkenlot, (5) five birds in a flock, (6) seven girls dancing, (7) a lady holding a pink parasol, (8) the parson holding a crooked staff, (9) the woodcutter with an axe, and (10) the cat (actually nine cats, beginning with a small pet cat, seven progressively fatter cats, and the final cat with a bandage on his stomach).

Optional Activities

Bag Fat Cats
Have the children color brown lunch bags and stuff them with old newspapers. Close the ends with rubber bands. The children can cut out feet and ears from construction paper and attach them to the paper bags. They can also draw facial features on the cat and attach black pipe cleaners for whiskers.

Materials needed:
- brown lunch bags
- construction paper
- rubber bands
- crayons
- black pipe cleaners
- old newspapers
- glue

Fat Cats on a Stick
Have each child blow up a balloon and tie it shut. Cut out ears and feet from construction paper, and attach to the balloon. Draw facial features and add whiskers using pipe cleaners or yarn. Attach a string to one end of a dowel rod and the other end to the balloon, and you have a "Fat Cat on a Stick."

Materials needed:
- balloons
- dowel rods
- string
- markers
- pipe cleaners or yarn
- construction paper

Preparation time
Story and figures: 25–40 min.
Optional Activities
  Bag Fat Cats: 10–20 min.
  Fat Cats on a Stick: 10–20 min.

Related Books: Greed

Berenstain, Stan and Jan. *The Berenstain Bears Get the Gimmies.* New York: Random House, 1988. The Bear family have to think of a way to help Brother and Sister Bear get rid of a bad case of the galloping greedy gimmies.

Galdone, Paul. *The Greedy Old Fat Man.* New York: Clarion, 1983. In this picturebook adaptation of an American folktale, a greedy old man eats anything he comes upon.

Rankin, Joan. *The Little Cat and the Greedy Old Woman.* New York: McElderry, 1995. The little cat gets revenge on the greedy old woman who refuses to share her special meal.

Remikiewicz, Frank. *Greedy Anna.* New York: Lothrop, Lee & Shepard, 1992. A family bends over backwards to accommodate Anna's "Mine! Mine! Mine!" phase.

Winthrop, Elizabeth. *That's Mine!* Illustrated by Emily McCully. New York: Holiday, 1977. Two children learn a lesson about sharing when they quarrel about blocks.

Grandpa Bud

by Siobhan Dodds
Candlewick, 1993

Summary: When Polly calls her grandpa and tells him she is coming to stay the night, he rushes around making the foods that she loves.

Procedure: Begin the session by telling the children that this story is about a little girl who plans to visit her grandpa. Ask the audience about visits that they have made to grandparents, aunts, or other special relatives. After discussing a few of the stories that the children relate, lead into *Grandpa Bud* by saying that Polly decides to bring some special friends along on her visit.

To make the characters and objects for the story, you can use a scanned or freehand picture of Grandpa Bud and Polly. The remainder of the characters can be made from felt with details added using markers or cutouts from magazines that have felt applied to the back.

Materials needed:
- assorted colors of felt
- glue
- scissors
- permanent markers

For the story, you will need the following flannelboard characters:

- Polly
- Grandpa Bud
- Henry (an animal)
- Rosie (stuffed duck)
- George (stuffed bear)
- Chocolate Cake
- Jello
- Ice Cream
- Banana Sandwiches
- Hot dogs

Use the illustrations in the book as a guide for the flannelboard figures.

Optional Activity

Special Friends

Everyone has a special toy, stuffed animal, or imaginary friend from their childhood. Ask the children to draw a picture of an object they feel is very special to them. Write a brief story about the special friend...

Related Books: Grandpa and Me

Hughes, Shirley. **When We Went to the Park.** New York: Lothrop, Lee & Shepard, 1985. While on a walk with her grandpa, a little girl counts the things in the park.

Mayer, Mercer. **Just Grandpa and Me.** New York: Golden, 1985. Little Critter and his grandpa go on a special trip to the city to buy a suit.

Stevenson, James. **We Can't Sleep.** New York: Greenwillow, 1983. Grandpa tells a long tale about the time when he couldn't sleep.

Tompert, Ann. **Grandfather Tang's Story.** Illustrated by Robert Andrew Parker. New York: Crown, 1990. As he tells a story about two foxes, Grandfather arranges Chinese puzzles to form the animals' shapes.

Preparation time
Story and figures: 1–2 hours
Optional Activities
    Special Friends: 5–15 min.

Humbug Witch
by Lorna Balian
Abingdon, 1965

Summary: A little witch cannot make her spells and potions work.

Procedure: This story is a good one to use with younger children near Halloween. Although it concerns a witch, the story is not scary and would not frighten younger children. Prior to the story session, place the witch figure in the center of the flannelboard, and turn the board so that the audience cannot see it. Introduce the story as a tale of a witch who cannot get her spells and potions to work. When you read the line, "You can see for yourself," turn the flannelboard around to face the audience. The only figure that you will add to the board is the black cat, Fred. As the witch removes her garments, remove pieces from the witch figure until only the little girl remains.

The base figure is made out of white felt with details added with markers. Many of the other items can be cut from felt or drawn on paper with the felt attached to the back. The stringy hair is a small wig made from yarn.

Materials needed:
- assorted colors of felt
- scissors
- yarn
- glue
- permanent markers

For the story, you will need the following felt items:
- base figure of a little girl
- tall pointed witch hat
- a broom
- two orange gloves
- black shoes with gold buckles
- stringy red hair
- plaid apron
- witch mask
- black shawl
- black cat

Optional Activities
I'm a Witch
Using black construction paper and tape, let each child create a witch's hat to take home.

Materials needed:
- black construction paper
- scissors
- tape

Just Hangin' Around
Each child can create a mobile to take home. Fold a piece of black construction paper in half, and cut out two witch hats. Cut a piece of string approximately 15" long and two small pieces approximately 3" long. Place the long string between the two hats, leaving 6½" at the top of the hat and 4½" at the bottom. Glue the string and two shapes together. Cut out eyes and a mouth. Attach the mouth to the short end of the string. Punch two holes in the hat, with one on each side of the mouth. Attach one end of the 3" string in the hole on one side of the hat and the other end in a small pinhole in the eye. Do the same for the other eye. If desired, use yarn or ribbon to give the witch some hair. Cut into 4" pieces.

If using ribbon for hair, you can curl it by running the dull edge of the scissors down the ribbon.

Materials needed:
- black and white construction paper
- scissors
- string
- ribbon and/or yarn
- glue and/or paste
- hole puncher

Preparation time
Story and figures: 1–2 hours
Optional Activities
   I'm a Witch: 10–15 min.
   Just Hangin' Around: 10–25 min.

Related Books: Witchy Tales

Adams, Adrienne. *A Woggle of Witches.* New York: Scribner, 1971. A group of witches set out to do some scaring, but they are the ones who end up frightened.

Buehner, Caralyn. *A Job for Wittilda.* Illustrated by Marc Buehner. New York: Dial, 1993. Wittilda gets a job delivering pizza in order to be able to feed her 47 cats.

Guthrie, Donna. *The Witch Who Lives Down the Hall.* New York: Harcourt, 1985. A little girl is sure that a witch is living down the hall in her apartment building.

Simmons, Steven J. *Slice and Greta.* Illustrated by Cyd Moore. Watertown, Mass.: Taleweeds, 1997. Two witches use their powers in very different ways, one helps people while the other creates mischief.

Stevenson, James. *Emma.* New York: Greenwillow, 1985. With the help of her friends and a few false starts, Emma learns to fly her broom.

Just Hangin' Around

Pattern for witch's hat

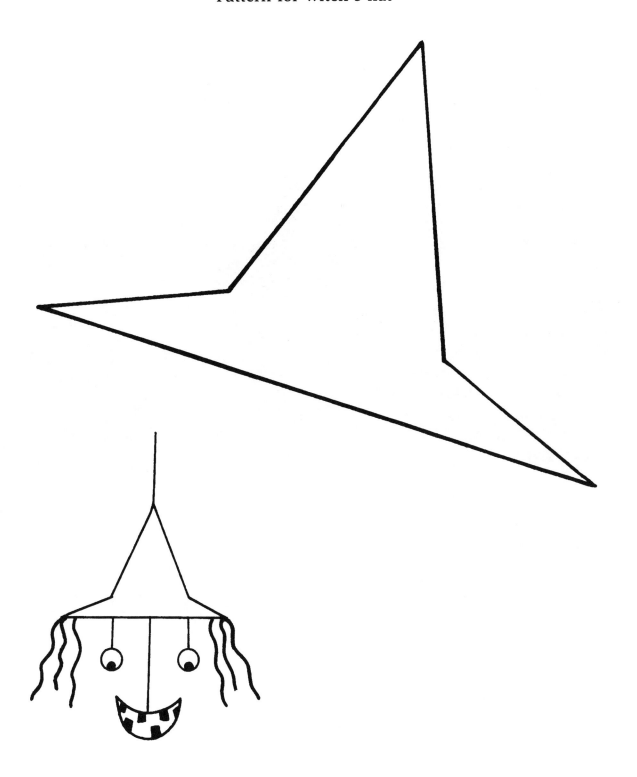

The Jacket I Wear in the Snow

By Shirley Neitzel • Illustrated by Nancy Winslow Parker
Greenwillow, 1989

Summary: In this cumulative tale, a little girl tells all the things that she puts on to go out to play in the snow.

Procedure: Begin by talking about winter and the many things associated with it: snow, cold, weather, icicles, red noses, and warm clothes. Lead into the story by saying this is a story about a little girl and what happens to her one winter day. Start by placing a figure of a little girl in the center of the board. As the story progresses, add clothing until the girl is ready to go out to play.

Materials needed:
- felt
- markers

Items needed for the story are:
- little girl
- jacket
- zipper
- jeans
- scarf
- long underwear
- mittens
- a mother
- doughnut
- cup
- sweater
- boots
- stocking cap
- tears

Optional Activities

What's the Weather Like Today

Make full-page patterns of different types of weather conditions. The patterns can include a snowflake for winter, a sun for summer, a raindrop for rainy weather, a cloud for stormy days, and other items that relate to weather. Give each child a pattern and have everyone write a story about the clothes that he or she wears in the _____. Using the rebus pattern found in the book create a simple story. The children can draw the clothing items or cut pictures from catalogs to add to the story.

Materials needed:
- paper
- old catalogs
- scissors
- glue
- markers, crayons, and pencils

What Happened to the Snow? (activity sheet)
Give each child a word scramble puzzle to take home. The puzzle contains all the items that the little girl wore in the snow.

Related Books: Winter Clothes

Brett, Jan. *The Mitten.* New York: Putnam, 1990. When Nicki loses a mitten in the snow, the forest animals use it to keep warm.

Munsch, Robert N. *Thomas' Snowsuit.* Illustrated by Michael Martchenko. Toronto: Annick, 1985. Thomas is determined not to wear the ugly brown snowsuit that his mother bought.

Nielsen, Laura F. *Jeremy's Muffler.* Illustrated by Christine M. Schneider. New York: Atheneum, 1995. When Jeremy's aunt knits him an extra long muffler and his mother makes him wear it, Jeremy's problems begin.

Spohn, Kate. *Clementine's Winter Wardrobe.* New York: Orchard, 1989. Clementine looks forward to a whole new wardrobe for the winter season.

Giveaway

"What Happened in the Snow?" activity sheet

 Preparation time
Story and figures: 40–75 min.
Optional Activities
What's the Weather Like Today?
15–30 min.
What Happened to the Snow?
5–15 min.

What Happened in the Snow?

Find all the things that happened to the little girl in the story *The Jacket I Wear in the Snow* by Shirley Neitzel. Circle the words that you find in the puzzle.

mittens   long underwear
zipper   stocking cap
scarf   jacket
sweater   socks
boots   jeans
mother   tears

```
L  O  N  G  U  N  D  E  R  W  E  A  R
L  O  B  O  O  T  S  G  B  M  N  S  E
M  I  N  D  E  S  O  C  K  S  V  Q  P
I  R  S  T  O  C  K  I  N  G  C  A  P
T  O  K  L  J  A  C  K  E  T  K  L  I
T  T  T  E  D  R  E  C  V  E  S  S  Z
E  F  A  D  V  F  C  B  S  A  C  N  M
N  N  A  D  M  O  T  H  E  R  V  L  Y
S  W  E  A  T  E  R  U  Y  S  E  H  J
```

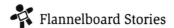

Old MacDonald Had an Apartment House

By Judith Barrett • Illustrated by John Barrett
Atheneum, 1969

Summary: Old MacDonald is the superintendent of an apartment building, but he would rather raise vegetables than fix broken pipes. When his tenants move out one by one, Old MacDonald turns each apartment into a garden plot until the entire building becomes a farm.

Procedure: As you give the title of the story, place the outline of an apartment building on the flannelboard. The three- or four-story building should cover most of the board, with windows cut out so that you can add things to the flannelboard as the story unravels. As the tenants move out of each of the apartments, add materials to the windows until you reach the point where the entire building turns into an indoor farm. At the end of the story, place a sign across the front of the building that reads, "WRENTAL & MACDONALD'S FRUITS & VEGETABLES."

Materials needed:
- assorted pieces of felt
- markers to outline and sketch on figures
- scissors

For the story you need to make (1) the outline of a large three- or four-story apartment building, (2) Old MacDonald, (3) Old MacDonald's wife, (4) fat Mr. Wrental, (5) a scarecrow, (6) a large-size tomato plant with small tomatoes on it, (7) a sign for the front of the building, and (8) items (to place in the windows) such as cows, chickens, cornstalks, sweet potato vines, mushrooms, cabbages, carrots, potatoes, pea vines, pigs, grass, and a few fruit trees.

Optional Activity

Old _____ Had a Farm (activity sheet)
On an activity sheet, each child can fill in the blank with his or her name. The activity sheet has the outline of a large apartment building on it. The children can fill in the windows with their ideas of what the steam-heated farm should have on it.

Related Books: Surviving Off the Land

French, Vivian. *Oliver's Vegetables*. Illustrated by Alisa Bartlett. New York: Orchard Books, 1995. When Oliver visits his grandfather, he discovers that vegetables are good to eat after all.

Krasilovsky, Phyllis. *The Man Who Cooked for Himself*. New York: Parents Magazine Press, 1981. When the man who lives at the edge of the woods eats all his food supply, he discovers all the good foods that grow in the natural environment.

McCloskey, Robert. *Blueberries for Sal*. New York: Viking, 1948. The story of a little girl and her mother who go blueberry picking and meet a mother bear and her cub.

Moore, Inga. *The Vegetable Thieves*. New York: Viking, 1984. Des and Letty are proud of their garden until the day their prize vegetables begin to disappear.

Westcott, Nadine Bernard. *The Giant Vegetable Garden*. Boston: Little, Brown, 1981. The townspeople grow the finest vegetables to win a prize at the fair.

 Preparation time
Story and figures: 1–2 hours
Optional Activities
   Old _____ Had a Farm: 5–15 min.

Old _____ Had a Farm

Draw pictures of what you might grow on a steam-heated apartment farm.

Fruits & Vegetables

The Very Busy Spider

by Eric Carle
Philomel, 1984

Summary: A busy little spider persists in spinning her web despite the farm animals' attempts to distract her.

Procedure: Because this story has very simple characters and a brief text, it makes an excellent flannelboard story. At the beginning of the story, place the spider and the sun on the board. Then, use yarn to build the little spider's web as the story progresses. The spider and her web occupy two-thirds of the board, with the farm animals and fly making their appearances on the remaining third. String the yarn in a pattern to make the web, fastening it with tape or thumbtacks. The fly appears with the entrance of the horse and stays on the board during the rest of the story. At the end, discuss how, why, and when spiders build webs. Give each child an activity sheet.

Materials needed:
- tape
- black marker
- felt in assorted colors
- scissors
- yarn for the web

Because these figures are so simple, all you need to do is to trace the shape of the animal from the text onto a piece of felt. Cut it out and add facial features and some shading. Cut yarn into manageable lengths.

Figures for the flannelboard include:
- spider
- pesky fly
- sheep
- pig
- cat
- rooster
- horse
- cow
- goat
- dog
- duck
- owl
- yellow sun

Instead of using yarn for the spider web, you can purchase a decorative spider web from a craft or fabric store. They are inexpensive and usually available near Halloween.

Optional Activities

The Spider and The Fly

Following the story and brief comments on spiders and web building, give each child a sheet of lightweight cardboard with a picture of the spider and the fly on it. By using glue and strands of string or yarn, each child can help the busy spider weave her web and catch the fly. If you do not want to use yarn, have children draw a web. For older children, give them a piece of cardboard and have them draw the spider and fly on it.

Materials needed:
- lightweight cardboard   yarn or string
- bottles of white glue   crayons or pencils
- paper towels (clean-up)   old newspapers

Complete the Web (activity sheet)

This simple activity is designed for preschoolers through first graders. It is a dot-to-dot puzzle that, when completed, is a picture of the spider and her web.

Related Books: Spiders

Graham, Margaret Bloy. *Be Nice to Spiders.* New York: Harper and Row, 1967. The zoo becomes a place of happiness and contentment when Billy donates his pet spider to them.

Kirk, David. *Miss Spider's Tea Party.* New York: Scholastic, 1994. Miss Spider has a party, but no one comes for fear of being eaten.

McDermott, Gerald. *Anansi the Spider; A Tale from the Ashanti.* New York: Holt, 1972. An African folktale about the adventures of Anansi the Spider.

Sardegna, Jill. *The Roly-Poly Spider.* Illustrated by Tedd Arnold. New York: Scholastic, 1994. A greedy, fat spider gets stuck in the water spout.

Giveaways

"Complete the Web" activity sheet and fact sheet

Preparation time
Story and figures: 1–3 hours
Optional Activities
The Spider and The Fly: 10–20 min.
Complete the Web: 3–5 min.

The Spider and the Fly

The spider is very busy. Can you help her make a web?

Complete the Web

Help the busy spider complete her web by connecting the dots 1 thru 48.

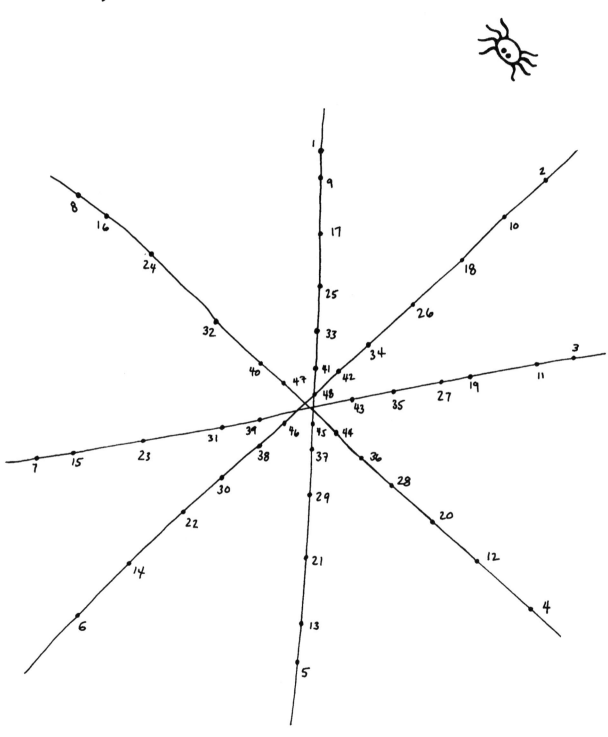

Did You Know?
(All about Spiders)

Physically speaking—

Spiders:

- have eight legs
- come in all shapes and sizes from as small as a pinhead to as big as 10 inches across
- do not have bones
- have fangs
- have eyes on top and near the front of their head
- have transparent blood

What they eat?

Insects, of course

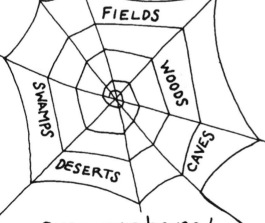

HOME is:

FIELDS

WOODS

SWAMPS

CAVES

DESERTS

...even your house! And anywhere they can find food.

Spider Facts

- Over 29,000 kinds of spiders are known to exist.
- Spiders are not insects—they are arachnids. (Ticks, mites, and scorpions are also in the arachnid category.)

Yummers

by James Marshall
Houghton Mifflin, 1973

Summary: Emily Pig tries to lose weight by exercising, but she finds herself sampling all the goodies that she encounters on her walk with Eugene Turtle.

Procedure: Explain that the title, *Yummers,* refers to things that are good to eat. Then, lead into the story of Emily Pig, who loves to eat and hates to exercise.

Materials needed:
- assorted scraps of felt
- black permanent markers

The flannelboard figures needed include: (1) Emily Pig, (2) Eugene Turtle, (3) a sandwich machine and some sandwiches, (4) a corn on the cob, (5) the tearoom and some scones, (6) an ice cream stand and Eskimo pies, (7) a box of Girl Scout cookies, (8) a vanilla malt, (9) a banana split, (10) a dish of peach ice cream, (11) a supermarket stand with pizza slices, (12) a park bench, (13) a bottle of cherry pop, and (14) a candied apple.

Make the flannelboard figures from assorted scraps of felt, and draw in details with the black permanent marker.

Optional Activities

Sensational Six

Give each child a sheet of lightweight cardboard containing a triangle divided into sections for each of the basic food groups. Have the children draw or cut out pictures of foods and place them in the correct food group.

As an alternative, provide the children with stickers of food or a picture sheet of various foods that they can place in the proper food group.

Materials needed:
- lightweight cardboard
- scissors
- glue and/or paste
- old magazines
- stickers or picture sheets (optional)

What Did Emily Eat? (activity sheet)

Give each child an activity sheet on which to circle the twelve different items that Emily ate while on her walk.

Related Books: We'll Eat Anything

Charlip, Remy, and Burton Supree. *"Mother, Mother I Feel Sick, Send for the Doctor Quick, Quick, Quick."* Illustrated by Remy Charlip. New York: Parents Magazine Press, 1966. A hilarious tale of a small boy with a most unusual stomachache.

Cole, Joanna. *Golly Gump Swallowed a Fly.* New York: Parents Magazine Press, 1981. Golly Gump accidentally swallows a variety of creatures and wins first prize as the best yawner.

Grossman, Bill. *My Sister Ate One Hare.* Illustrated by Kevin Hawkes. New York: Crown, 1996. A little girl eats snakes, ants, and even lizards, but when it comes to peas, she throws up quite a mess.

Marshall, James. *Yummers Too: A Second Course.* Boston: Houghton Mifflin, 1986. When Emily Pig tries to earn some money to pay off her debts created by her love of food, she finds her appetite keeps getting in the way.

Taback, Simms. *There Was an Old Lady Who Swallowed a Fly.* New York: Viking, 1997. In this new version of a well-loved poem, the reader gets a glimpse at what went on inside the old lady's stomach.

Preparation time
Story and figures: 1–3 hours
Optional Activities
  Sensational Six: 10–20 min.
  What Did Emily Eat? 5–15 min.

Sensational Six

Draw or cut out pictures of foods that belong in each of the
six food groups and place them in the proper category.

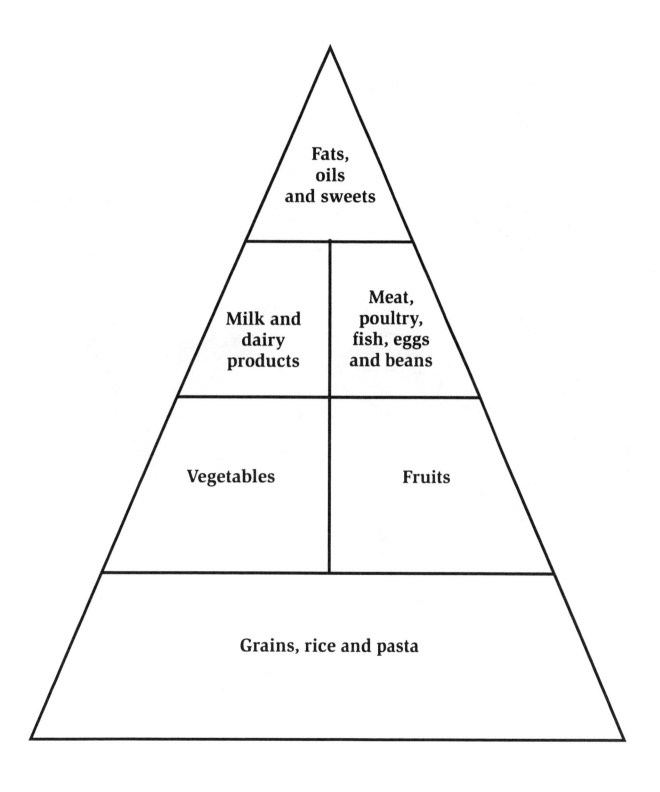

What Did Emily Eat?

Circle the foods that Emily ate on her walk with Eugene Turtle.

✋ *Participation Storytelling*

Over the past few years, the genre of interactive fiction, videos, computer games, and online games has become very popular, and participation storytelling is a natural extension to this trend. In fact, storytellers have always used a form of interactive participation to add variety and excitement to a story session.

Unlike traditional storytelling methods, participation storytelling requires active physical responses from the listeners. The audience uses voice and body movements to express action and sounds in the story. Simple participation storytelling takes place when the children repeat a phrase or action in the story either spontaneously or on cue. More complex forms of participation storytelling require costumes and assigned lines. Creative dramatics using more elaborate participation are a natural extension of a story, especially with older children.

Because this type of storytelling invites the audience into the story and increases enjoyment, it can be rewarding both for the storyteller and for the listener. The children become involved in the action of the story and feel that they are a part of it. They can derive satisfaction and a sense of self-esteem from the opportunity to perform before others. Participation storytelling is an enjoyable way for a group to relax after a stressful class and provides another medium of presentation for the storyteller.

Stories that contain repeated refrains, chants, songs, or chances for movement, noisemaking, or clapping are naturals to use in participation storytelling. However, many stories can be adapted for use, ranging from spontaneous or cued repetition of keywords or key phrases to more complex puppetry and dramatics.

Approaches to Participation Storytelling

A story can be tailored for listener participation through a variety of methods and combinations of movement, speaking, chanting, singing, and noisemaking. The simplest approach is a spontaneous group reaction from the audience, where the children chime in with a repetitive phrase or refrain and enjoy the idea that they are helping you read. By choosing a story that repeats a keyword or key phrase throughout the action, you will often find that children provide an automatic response. For example, in *What Can You Do with a Kangaroo?* by Mercer Mayer, by the second or third time that you ask the title question, most of the children will respond with the key phrase, "Throw him out." Any story with a repetitive phrase or refrain is good to use with this approach, including such tales as *Millions of Cats* by Wanda Gag, *Brown Bear, Brown Bear, What Do You See?* by Bill Martin, and *The Little Engine that Could* by Watty Piper.

Another approach is to have the children listen for keywords or key phrases that they repeat on cue or to have them provide the answer to a question. You can either tell the entire group a phrase to repeat on cue such as "I don't know why . . . Perhaps she'll die" from *I Know an Old Lady Who Swallowed a Fly* or assign words or sounds to individual children. *The Grouchy Ladybug* by Eric Carle is a good story to use with this approach. Make stick puppets for each of the animals the ladybug encounters, and give a puppet to selected children, telling them to respond to a question with the words, "If you insist." Giving responses on cue is a good technique to use with all age groups and provides a less threatening situation. Cumulative tales are especially good for this approach, especially stories such as *The Fat Cat* retold by Jack Kent, *A Fly Went By* by Mike McClintock, *The House that Jack Built*, and *The Rose in My Garden* by Arnold Lobel.

A third approach for participation storytelling is dramatization acted out before an audience. You may choose to give children nonspeaking or speaking parts. Dramatization helps children visualize a story but prevents embarrassment for those who will not or cannot read a part. With younger children, give nonspeaking action or sound parts. *Stone Soup* by Marcia Brown is a good story to use for a nonspeaking dramatization. Each child is given an item to add to the soup and needs only to bring it forth to put in the kettle rather than actually to speak a part in the story.

You can plan movements for the audience during the story by using (1) natural gestures such as nodding, smiling, or clapping or (2) invented movements such as bowing heads or throwing up hands when the storyteller gives a cue. Other stories that are good to use for nonspeaking parts include: *The Great Big Enormous Turnip* by Aleksei Tolstoi, *The Old Woman and Her Pig* illustrated by Paul Galdone, *It Could Always Be Worse* by Margot Zemach, and *Jump, Frog, Jump!* by Robert Kalan.

Having a child perform a speaking part is a big step and is a more threatening situation for the child than just having him or her provide a sound on cue. Involving the audience in speaking parts can range from (1) very simple question and answer responses to (2) dividing the audience into two groups that play one or more characters to (3) the more complex process of wearing costumes, practicing lines, and presenting the story as a drama. Some stories that are good for creative dramatics include *George and Martha* by James Marshall, *The Worst Person in the World* by James Stevenson, and *The Little Engine that Could*.

Sound Effect Stories

In addition to action participation, the storyteller can use sounds as a part of the program. Sound effects created by the audience can enhance a story. The action of a character or object in the story may spark a sound or the sound effects may be a part of the text itself. Sound effects can be created in a variety of ways including by vocally making noises such as mooing, clucking, or laughing; by physically making noises by snapping fingers, stomping feet, or snoring; by using found objects to create noises such as jangling keys, crumbling paper, or tapping a pencil; and by using musical instruments such as drums, cymbals, or rhythm sticks to create sounds.

In using the story *The Little Old Lady Who Was Not Afraid of Anything* by Linda Williams, you can assign sounds to various children in the audience. Each child produces a sound on cue, thus providing a form of group dramatics. By the time that you reach the final stages of the story, all of the children know the sounds and are recreating them with you.

Another example of a story in which you can use sound effects is *Tikki Tikki Tembo* retold by Arlene Mosel. You can give the children found objects or musical instruments to use when repeating the refrain, "Tikki-tikki-tembo, no-sa-rembo, chari-bari-ruchi-pip-peri-pembo." The children can, for example, beat a drum, shake a box of dried beans, or pound together wooden spoons. Other good sound effect stories are *One Fine Day* by Nonny Hogrogian, *The Camel Who Took a Walk* by Jack Tworkow, and *The Brave Little Indian* retold by Bill and Bernard Martin.

Choosing Stories and Participants

The storyteller should maintain control of the story at all times. Choose stories that let the storyteller carry the main role while the children have supplemental or supporting roles. It is also important to be careful in selecting the participants. In choosing a child, consider whether the child can read, gets stage fright, speaks in a low voice, or might decide to do his or her own thing rather than the assigned task.

Participation storytelling can be fun and is a nice change of pace for both the storyteller and the listener. It is an interesting medium to use to present literature to children.

Another Mouse to Feed

By Robert Kraus • Illustrated by Jose Aruego & Ariane Dewey
Windmill, 1980

Summary: When a new baby arrives on the doorstep, Mr. and Mrs. Mouse and their 31 children all have to pitch in to help around the house.

Procedure: Begin the story session by bringing forth a large yellow box painted or covered with paper to resemble a piece of Swiss cheese. Cut several holes in the box, and dangle pieces of gray yarn from the holes. As you begin the story, introduce Mr. and Mrs. Mouse to the audience by having one of the children pull the two largest pieces of yarn from the box. On the end of the yarn, the children will find Mr. and Mrs. Mouse. Throughout the story, let each child pull on the dangling tails to reveal the entire mouse family to the group. When the baby mouse enters the story, introduce him by bringing out a small box decorated to look like a baby bed, instead of pulling him out of the box.

Follow up the story with a discussion on the kinds of jobs the children's parents have that take them outside of the home each day.

Materials needed:
- large box (covered with yellow paper or painted yellow)
- scissors
- gray and pink felt
- glue and/or rubber cement
- gray yarn
- moveable eyes (32 small pairs and 2 large pairs)
- needle and thread
- small box (matchbox size)
- small plastic toy mice (optional)
- large pom-poms (optional)

The cheese box and mice take quite a bit of time to make, depending on how complex you want them to be. Take a large cardboard box, and cut small holes around it to resemble a block of Swiss cheese. Paint the box yellow or cover it with paper. You will need to make small cardboard shelves to attach to the inside of the box to sit the mouse puppets on.

You can make the mice from felt or large pom-poms or even use small plastic toy mice available from toy or department stores. If you make felt finger puppets or pom-pom mice, you can individualize the mice using ribbons, whiskers, or minicostumes.

Mr. and Mrs. Mouse should be made from felt and be larger than their children.

For the felt finger puppets, cut out two small mouse shapes and sew them together, leaving the bottom open. Add wiggle eyes, a felt nose, and yarn whiskers to complete the puppet. Attach a tail with the gray yarn. Be sure the tails are long enough to hang out of the box openings.

To make pom-pom mice, cut out ears and feet from felt. Glue moveable eyes and the felt parts on a large pom-pom. Attach a long tail to the mouse.

If desired, decorate the puppets with materials such as ribbons, minicostumes, and beads.

Optional Activities

Pom-Pom Mice

Cut out ears, tails, and feet from felt, and glue these parts onto a large pom-pom. Attach moveable wiggle eyes.

Materials needed:
- large pom-poms
- felt
- small wiggle eyes
- scissors
- glue

Swiss Cheese Bookmarks

Give the children sheets of yellow construction

> **Preparation time**
> Story and mouse theater: 1–2 hours
> **Optional Activities**
> Pom-Pom Mice: 5–15 min.
> Swiss Cheese Bookmarks: 5–15 min.

paper and scissors. Let them cut strips of paper for bookmarks. Cut holes in the strips to resemble Swiss cheese, and decorate the rest of the bookmark.

Materials needed:
- scissors
- yellow construction paper
- markers and/or crayons

Related Books: Mice in the House

Freeman, Don. ***Norman the Doorman***. New York: Viking, 1959. The story of Norman, who works as a doormouse at the Art Museum.

Gurney, Nancy, and Eric Gurney. ***The King, the Mice, and the Cheese***. Illustrated by Jean Vallier. New York: Random House, 1965. A king tries to keep the mice from eating his food.

Holl, Adelaide. ***Moon Mouse***. New York: Random House, 1973. When Arthur sees the moon for the first time, he decides to find out if the moon is made of cheese.

Kraus, Robert. ***Big Squeak, Little Squeak***. Pictures by Kevin O'Malley. New York: Orchard, 1996. Two mice venture into a cheese shop and battle a big cat.

Lionni, Leo. ***Matthew's Dream***. New York: Knopf, 1991. When Matthew visits the art museum, he discovers the answer to his dream.

Steig, William. ***Doctor De Soto***. New York: Farrar, Straus & Giroux, 1982. A mouse dentist has to be careful about his patients.

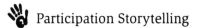

Glad Monster Sad Monster
A Book About Feelings

by Ed Emberley and Anne Miranda

Little, Brown, 1997

Summary: The colorful monsters show the reader how they express their feelings.

Procedures: Introduce this book by saying that sometimes it is hard to tell someone how you feel. The monsters in the book talk about the things that make them feel happy or sad or worried. Each double-page spread includes a fold-out flap that has a monster mask on it. Choose seven children from the audience to help with the story. Each child will fold out the mask and pretend to exhibit the feelings of the monster. After each child pretends to be a monster, ask him or her to tell things that make them feel just like that monster.

Optional Activities

Feely Faces

Tell the children they are going to make feely face masks. Each child will decorate a paper plate to reflect a feeling or emotion. For example, an angry feely face might be deep red, have a big frown, and have scraggly hair; a grouchy face might be covered with fur like a bear, have a scrunched up mouth and tightly woven hair. Tell the children to use their imaginations to create their face masks. Punch holes on each side of the paper plate, attach elastic string, and wear the faces.

Materials needed:
- paper plates
- coloring medium
- scraps of materials, felt, paper, and fake fur
- glue
- scissors
- elastic string
- paper punch

Monster Faces

The Monster Faces game can be adapted to play with any age. Divide the group into two equal teams. Explain that you are going to name an emotion, and the teams have to decide how to make a monster face with that emotion. The team who makes the best face gets a point. At the end of the game, the team with the most points wins a prize. Prizes can be happy face stickers, pencils, or other items.

Materials needed:
- list of emotions
- prizes, such as happy face stickers, pencils, etc.

How Do I Feel?

Make up an activity sheet filled with six to nine circles to represent faces. Have the children draw different emotions on the circles to demonstrate feelings like the monsters in the book. Under each circle, have them list several things that make them feel like the face that was drawn.

Related Books: What a Feeling!

Aliki. *Feelings.* New York: Greenwillow, 1984. Poetry, stories, cartoons, and dialogue are used to show all sorts of emotions.

Anholt, Catherine and Laurence. *What I Like.* New York: Putnam, 1991. Six children take turns telling all the things that they like and dislike.

Boyton, Sandra. *A Is for Angry.* New York: Workman, 1983. In this ABC book, each letter of the alphabet stands for an emotion.

 Preparation time
Story and props: 30–60 min.
Optional Activities
   Feely Faces: 10–30 min.
   Monster Faces: 10–20 min.
   How Do I Feel? 10–20 min.

Monster Faces

Use this list of emotions and feelings to play the Monster Faces game.

angry	frustrated	nervous
anxious	furious	
ashamed		overwhelmed
	glad	
bored	grief	pouty
brave	guilt	proud
cautious	happy	quiet
confident	hate	
confused	hopeful	sad
	hysterical	scary
depressed		selfish
disgusted	impatient	shocked
	insulted	shy
ecstatic		silly
embarrassed	jealous	smug
enraged		stubborn
envy	lonely	surprised
exhausted	loving	suspicious
	lovestruck	
fat		worried
fear	mischievous	
frightened		

The Grouchy Ladybug

by Eric Carle
Crowell, 1986

Summary: The ladybug spends the day bullying and badgering everyone she meets until finally at sunset she encounters her match.

Procedure: To introduce the story, comment on feeling bad and how sometimes we all have changeable moods. Lead into the story by talking about the ladybug's grouchy mood. As you are talking, pass out puppets to twelve children in the front of the group. Tell these children that they are going to help out with the story. When you name the character that the child is holding, have the child stand up, hold the puppet up high, and answer your question with the words, "If you insist." Then, the child should sit down.

Materials needed:
- 15 paper plates
- craft sticks
- felt-tipped markers
- masking tape

Trace the outline of each animal in the story onto a paper plate. Number the back of the puppets in the order of their appearance in the story. Using the markers, fill in the details of the animals. Use masking tape to attach a craft stick for a holder onto the bottom of each plate.

You will need the following puppets: (1) a yellow jacket, (2) a stag beetle, (3) a praying mantis, (4) a sparrow, (5) a lobster, (6) a skunk, (7) a boa constrictor, (8) a laughing hyena, (9) a gorilla, (10) a rhinoceros, (11) an elephant (which requires two paper plates glued together), and (12) a whale (which requires three paper plates glued together lengthwise).

Optional Activities

Clay Ladybugs

Children can create their own ladybugs out of clay. After molding the basic shape of the ladybug, paint it red. Use a fast drying paint, so the project can be completed in one session. When the red paint is dry, use black paint to add details such as eyes, spots, etc. If desired, coat the final product with clear spray to make the ladybug shine.

Materials needed:
- modeling clay
- red and black paint (quick-drying latex enamel)
- paintbrushes
- old newspapers
- clear acrylic spray (optional)

Bouncing Paper Ladybugs

Cut a ladybug body from red construction paper. Draw spots and other features on the ladybug with crayons or markers. Accordion fold the strips of black construction paper for the ladybug's legs. Attach legs to the body with glue, tape, or staples. Attach a string to the center of the ladybug's back.

Materials needed:
- red and black construction paper
- crayons or markers
- string
- tape, glue, or staples

 Preparation time
Story and puppets: 40–45 min.
Optional Activities
   Clay Ladybugs: 20–30 min.
   Bouncing Paper Ladybugs: 15–25 min.

Related Books: Temper Tantrums

Berridge, Celia. *Hannah's Temper*. New York: Scholastic, 1992. Hannah is having a very bad day where everything seems to go wrong.

Blumenthal, Deborah. *The Chocolate-Covered Cookie Tantrum*. Pictures by Harvey Stevenson. New York: Clarion, 1996. When Sophie sees a girl in the park with a cookie, she throws a fit to get one for herself.

Preston, Edna Mitchell. *The Temper Tantrum Book*. New York: Viking, 1969. All the animals throw temper tantrums.

Simon, Norma. *I Was So Mad*. Illustrated by Joseph Leon Lasker. Chicago: Albert Whitman, 1974. This is a book all about things that make you mad.

Zolotow, Charlotte. *The Quarrelling Book*. Illustrated by Arnold Lobel. New York: Harper and Row, 1963. In this book, a family learns that anger and kindness can be contagious.

I Unpacked My Grandmother's Trunk

by Susan Ramsey Hoguet
Dutton, 1983

Summary: Objects from A to Z emerge from grandmother's trunk in this picturebook version of an old memory game.

Procedure: Introduce the story by bringing out a box decorated to look like an old trunk. You can use an old wooden cigar box or a jewelry box instead of a trunk. As you begin, open the lid and take out a card with a picture of the first item (an acrobat). Give the card to a child, and have the child stand up holding the card. Continue with the rest of the rhyme, giving each card to a different child, who in turn stands up and becomes a part of the circle. As you add new items, have the children repeat the preceding list each time until all 26 items are revealed.

This is a good exercise to use when a large class visits the library.

If desired, you can also present this story as a game. Directions are found in the picture book.

When you are finished with the rhyme, let the children think of and name other items that might have been in the trunk.

Materials needed:
- box decorated to look like an old trunk
- lightweight cardboard
- coloring medium
- pictures of the 26 items found in the trunk

Optional Activity

What Else Was in the Trunk?

Give the children small index cards, and explain that just as the rhyme named things from A to Z, the children are to create a set of memory cards of items from A to Z. The pictures can be drawn on the cards, or the children can cut out pictures from old magazines and newspapers.

Materials needed:
- small index cards
- old magazines and/or newspapers
- pencils, markers, and crayons
- scissors
- glue and/or paste

Related Books: ABCs

Bayer, Jane. *A My Name Is Alice.* New York: Dial, 1987. A picturebook version of a jumping rope rhyme.

Darling, Kathy. *Amazon ABC.* Photographs by Tara Darling. New York: Lothrop, Lee & Shepard, 1996. From red-tail boa to pygmy marmosets, this book offers an A to Z tour of the Amazon rainforest.

Johnson, Stephen T. *Alphabet City.* New York: Viking, 1995. This wordless book uses photographs to show how letters can be found in familiar objects.

Lobel, Arnold. *On Market Street.* New York: Greenwillow, 1981. A little girl goes shopping for gifts from A to Z.

MacDonald, Suse. *Alphabatics.* New York: Bradbury, 1987. The letters of the alphabet are gradually transformed into familiar objects and animals.

Preparation time
Story and props: 1–2 hours
Optional Activities
What Else Was in the Trunk?
10–30 min.

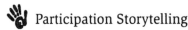

The Little Old Lady Who Was Not Afraid of Anything

by Linda Williams
Crowell, 1986

Summary: A series of spooky things scare "the little old lady" who was not afraid of anything as she returns from a walk in the woods.

Procedure: After the children are seated, explain that they are going to help tell the story. Give one child a bag filled with pebbles or some other substance that he or she can shake. Tell the children to stomp their feet when you say "clomp, clomp"; clap their hands when you say "clap, clap"; and nod their heads when you say "nod, nod." The child holding the bag is to shake it when you say "shake, shake."

The story has a series of sounds and actions that are repeated as the tale unfolds. When you say that shoes went "clomp, clomp," children stomp their feet; pants went "wiggle, wiggle," children wiggle in their seats; shirt went "shake, shake," one child shakes a bag of pebbles; two white gloves went "clap, clap," children clap their hands; a hat went "nod, nod," children nod their heads; and a head went "boo, boo," everyone yells "Boo!" For the last sound, the knock at the door, just knock against the chair or bookcase.

For the finale, bring out a scarecrow puppet or cardboard figure.

Materials needed:
- paper bag filled with pebbles or another item to shake
- scarecrow puppet or cardboard figure

Optional Activities

Paper Bag Scarecrows
Give each child a brown paper lunch bag to fill with crumpled newspapers. Place a small dowel rod through the stuffed bag and tie up the end of the bag with a string or a rubber band. Turn the bag upside down and decorate the scarecrow. Use crayons, paint, or markers to make facial features and clothing. Use yarn scraps for hair. Construct a hat from paper.

Materials needed:
- brown paper lunch bags
- yarn scraps

- old newspapers
- string or rubber bands
- assorted colors of construction paper
- markers, crayons, or paint
- small dowel rods

Let's Make Scarecrows (activity sheet)
Give each preschooler or kindergartner an activity sheet with the outline of a person on it. Each child can add facial features and clothing to create a scarecrow.

Related Books: Scarecrows

Fleishman, Sid. *The Scarebird.* Illustrated by Peter Sis. New York: Greenwillow, 1988. A young man helps a lonely farmer build his scarecrow.

Gordon, Sharon. *Sam the Scarecrow.* Mahwah, NJ: Troll, 1981. This book is an easy-to-read tale about a scarecrow.

Littlewood, Valerie. *Scarecrow!* New York: Dutton, 1992. Littlewood chronicles the legends and lore of the scarecrow.

Rylandt, Cynthia. *Scarecrow.* Illustrated by Lauren Stringer. Orlando: Harcourt Brace, 1998. A scarecrow enjoys his peaceful life surrounded by nature.

Schlerte, Alice. *Witch Hazel.* Illustrated by Margot Tomes. New York: HarperCollins, 1991. Johnny uses a witch hazel branch for his scarecrow and is amazed when it comes to life.

Giveaway
"Let's Make Scarecrows" (activity sheet)

 Preparation time
Story: 10–15 min.
Optional Activities
 Paper Bag Scarecrows: 10–25 min.
 Let's Make Scarecrows: 5–10 min.

Let's Make Scarecrows

Draw a scarecrow like the one that followed the little old lady home.

Millions of Cats

by Wanda Gag
Coward, 1928

Summary: The story is about a man who searches for one small cat and finds himself with millions of them.

Procedure: Introduce the story by talking about cats. Ask the group if anyone has a cat. If so, how does it behave? What does it look like? Lead into the story by stating that it is about a man in search of a cat. Explain that there is a phrase repeated throughout the story that you want the children to say with you. Say the phrase "hundreds of cats, thousands of cats, millions and billions and trillions of cats" and have the children repeat it after you.

When you have finished reading or telling the story, ask the group to think of a name for the little cat who becomes a pet.

Optional Activities

Clever Cats (activity sheet)

Let the children cut out cat figures from construction paper and decorate them. Then, have the children name their cats and use the figures to decorate a bulletin board entitled "Clever Cats," or hang the cat figures on a tree branch set in a pot. Surround the branch with a display of books about cats or a collection of jackets from books about cats.

Materials needed:
- construction paper
- scissors
- crayons and/or markers
- tree branch set in a bucket or pot (optional)
- string (optional)

Cat Puzzles

Copy cat scenes from the story, or draw cat figures on sheets of paper. Mount the pictures on cardboard, and cover them with contact paper. Cut the scenes into several puzzle pieces. Place the puzzle pieces into envelopes for the children to take home, so that each child has a complete puzzle.

Materials needed:
- lightweight cardboard
- scissors
- glue and/or paste
- contact paper
- crayons and/or markers
- envelopes

Related Materials: Kitty Cats

Dils, Tracey E. *Cat Characters – A to Z.* Illustrations by Mimi Vang Olsen. New York: American Editions, 1995. Cats with names from A to Z are presented in this beautifully illustrated book.

Keats, Ezra Jack. *Hi Cat!* New York: Macmillan, 1970. A mischievous stray cat disrupts Archie and his friends at play.

Newberry, Clare Turlay. *Marshmallow.* New York: Harper, 1942. Oliver, the cat, and Marshmallow, the rabbit, become best friends.

Pilkey, Dav. *When Cats Dream.* New York: Orchard, 1992. The dreams of cats are more colorful than reality.

Pittman, Helena Clare. *Miss Hindy's Cats.* Minneapolis: Carolrhoda, 1990. From A to Z, Miss Hindy has to find names for all the cats that move in with her.

Preparation time
Story: 5–15 min.
Optional Activities
Clever Cats 5–15 min.
Cat Puzzles 5–15 min.

Clever Cats

The Mitten

By Alvin Tresselt • Illustrated by Yaroslava
Lothrop, Lee & Shepard, 1964

Summary: When a little boy loses his mitten in the woods, a number of animals take refuge in the mitten to escape the cold and snow.

Procedure: As you announce the name of the story, bring out a very large plastic garbage bag, and explain to the children that they are going to help you tell the story. Pass out masks to several of the children and explain that the garbage bag represents a mitten lost in the woods. Each child with a mask comes to the front of the group when his or her character appears in the story. As the story progresses, the children try to squeeze into the bag just as the animals do in the story. When the child who is the cricket tries to get in the bag, it splits.

Materials needed:
- paper plates
- markers
- construction paper
- scissors
- glue and/or paste
- yarn
- elastic string

One mask is needed for each of the following characters: mouse, rabbit, wild boar, frog, fox, bear, owl, big gray wolf, and small black cricket.

To make the masks, draw the facial features of the animal on the front of a paper plate. Color in the features, and add lines and more details with a black felt-tipped marker. Cut ears, noses, and other features from construction paper, and attach these features to the paper plate. Use yarn, string, or pipe cleaners for whiskers and hair, and attach them to the plate. Punch a hole on each side of the plate, and attach a piece of elastic string on the sides.

Optional Activity

Who Wants to Get into the Mitten? (activity sheet)

Using the activity sheet, each child is to draw all of the animals that want to get into the mitten.

Related Books: Lost Mittens

Brett, Jan. *The Mitten.* New York: Putnam, 1990. This beautifully illustrated book is another version of the Ukraine folktale about a mitten that serves as a home for several forest animals.

Kay, Helen. *One Mitten Lewis.* Illustrated by Kurt Wiese. New York: Lothrop, Lee & Shepard, 1968. Lewis loses so many mittens that he has to wear mismatched ones, and all his friends call him One-Mitten Lewis.

Kellogg, Steven. *The Mystery of the Missing Red Mitten.* New York: Dial, 1974. When the red mitten disappears, no one is able to find it until spring.

Rogers, Jean. *Runaway Mittens.* Illustrated by Rie Munoz. New York: Greenwillow, 1988. Pica's mittens seem to always disappear by themselves.

Slobodkin, Florence, and Louis S. Slobodkin. *Too Many Mittens.* New York: Vanguard, 1958. Everyone in the neighborhood brings a pair of mittens to hang on the "Lost Mitten Line."

 Preparation time
Story and masks: 30–90 min.
Optional Activities
Who Wants to Get Into the Mitten?
5–15 min.

Who Wants to Get into the Mitten?

Draw pictures of all the animals who wanted to get into the mitten.

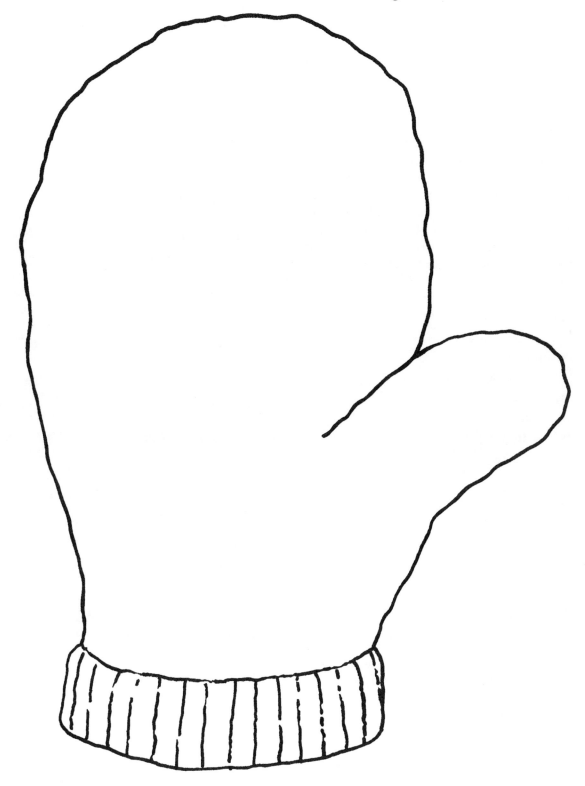

The Philharmonic Gets Dressed

By Karla Kuskin • Illustrated by Marc Simont

Harper and Row, 1982

Summary: In this story, the 105 members of the Philharmonic get dressed and ready for a Friday evening performance.

Procedure: Introduce the story by talking about getting dressed and ready for school or for work each day. Discuss how we all choose clothes to fit the occasion. Lead into the story by bringing out a box filled with instruments made from everyday items. Pass out the instruments, and tell the group that just as the members of the Philharmonic are getting ready for a performance, they are going to get ready for a performance by listening to the story.

Proceed to tell the story. Afterward, let the children practice with the instruments and pretend to be members of an orchestra.

Homemade instruments to include:
- spoons
- tongue depressors
- pots and pans
- tissue paper
- aluminum pie plates
- plastic dishes
- sandpaper
- empty soup cans
- ring of keys

Optional Activities

Make Your Own Music

As an accompaniment to the story, have the children make instruments to take home with them. All of the following are easily made from everyday items: horns from cardboard tubes with holes cut in them at various intervals, drums from empty boxes such as oatmeal boxes covered with paper, cymbals from two aluminum pie plates, tambourines from a bunch of old keys on a key ring, shakers from a container half filled with dry macaroni or beans, and sticks from two tongue depressors or wooden spoons.

Materials needed:
- cardboard tubes
- empty boxes
- aluminum pie plates
- keys and key rings
- dry macaroni and/or beans
- tongue depressors
- wooden spoons

What Is It?

Mount pictures of musical instruments on 8½"x11" sheets of white cardboard. Place the pictures around the area, and let the children try to identify them. Be sure to write the answers on the back of the sheets.

A good place to find nice drawings and illustrations is in *Music*, from the Eyewitness Books series published by Knopf.

Materials needed:
- white cardboard (8½"x11")
- illustrations and/or drawings of musical instruments

Music in the Air (activity sheet)

This drawing sheet is designed for children in preschool through grade 1.

Find the Instruments (activity sheet)

Find the instruments in the word puzzle and circle them.

Preparation time

Story and instruments: 1–2 hours

Optional Activities

Make Your Own Music: 10–30 min.

What Is It? 5–15 min.

Music in the Air: 5–10 min.

Find the Instruments: 5–15 min.

Related Books: Time to Get Dressed

Carlstrom, Nancy White. *Jesse Bear, What Will You Wear?* Illustrated by Bruce Degen. New York: Macmillan, 1986. A rhyming story of a bear getting dressed and undressed.

Kuskin, Karla. *The Dallas Titans Get Ready for Bed.* Illustrated by Marc Simont. New York: Harper and Row, 1986. In this sequel to *The Philharmonic Gets Dressed,* the reader learns all about the equipment, clothing, and preparations of a football team.

Neitzel, Shirley. *The Dress I'll Wear to the Party.* Pictures by Nancy Winslow Parker. New York: Greenwillow, 1992. A little girl describes dressing up in her mother's party things.

Peek, Merle. *Mary Wore a Red Dress and Henry Wore His Green Sneakers.* New York: Clarion, 1983. In this story which is based on a traditional folk song, each animal wears a different color to a birthday party.

Wells, Rosemary. *Max's New Suit.* New York: Dial, 1979. When Max's sister Ruby tries to dress him for a party, Max takes matters into his own hands and dresses himself.

Giveaway

An information sheet about musical instruments

Music in the Air

Where is the music coming from?
Draw some of the instruments and musicians you see in an orchestra.

Find the Instruments

All of the 105 members of the orchestra are getting ready to go to work where they will play beautiful music. Circle the names of their instruments in the word scramble below. You may circle words up, down, across and backward, and diagonally to find all 18 instruments.

```
F  R  E  N  C  H  H  O  R  N  S  C
E  R  L  N  L  V  I  O  L  A  E  Y
B  W  G  M  A  I  W  Z  L  L  N  M
A  E  N  C  R  O  W  Q  L  M  O  B
S  F  A  H  I  L  B  O  T  U  B  A
S  G  I  I  N  I  L  O  M  D  M  L
O  T  R  M  E  N  X  C  E  O  O  S
O  R  T  E  T  E  W  I  C  M  R  W
N  U  W  S  L  D  I  F  L  U  T  E
S  M  U  R  D  Z  C  L  R  H  I  C
V  P  I  C  C  O  L  O  A  T  R  E
K  E  T  T  L  E  D  R  U  M  S  O
R  T  M  C  E  T  P  Y  U  I  N  X
```

bassoon	flute	triangle
cello	french horn	trombones
chimes	harp	trumpet
clarinet	kettle drums	tuba
cymbals	oboe	viola
drums	piccolo	violin

Stone Soup

Text and illustrations by Marcia Brown
Scribner, 1947

Summary: Three hungry soldiers manage to convince the unfriendly townspeople to contribute ingredients to a pot of delicious stone soup.

Procedure: Seat the children in a semicircle with one open end where you will sit. Place a large black kettle in the center of the circle in front of you. Introduce the story by telling the children that they are going to help you to tell it. After you give each child one of the ingredients for the stone soup, explain that when the story calls for that ingredient the child should bring it to the front of the group and add it to the stone soup.

Materials needed:
- Large black pot or kettle (can use plastic black pots available from stores that sell flower pots)

Ingredients for soup:
- empty milk and/or water containers (for buckets of water)
- 3 medium-sized stones
- real salt and pepper shakers with or without seasonings in them
- real carrots and potatoes
- cardboard or plastic barley, cabbages, and meat
- empty milk cartons

Optional Activity

Make a Pot of Stone Soup (activity sheet)
Give each child an activity sheet containing the outline of a large pot in the center. The children are to draw ingredients that would be added to the pot to make a pot of stone soup.

Related Books: Anyone for a Cup of Soup?

Everitt, Betsy. *Mean Soup.* San Diego: Harcourt, 1992. Cranky Horace has a change of mood after he makes mean soup with his mother.

Hale, Linda. *The Glorious Christmas Soup Party.* New York: Viking, 1962. When the mouse family faces Christmas with nothing to eat, their friends drop by with food presents to put in the soup pot.

Orgel, Doris. *Button Soup.* Art by Paul Estrada. New York: Bantam, 1994. The whole neighborhood pitches in to make button soup.

Stevenson, James. *Yuck!* New York: Greenwillow, 1984. When Emma is ignored by the older witches, she cooks up a soup of her own with an extra special ingredient.

Zemach, Harve. *Nail Soup.* Illustrated by Margot Zemach. Chicago: Follett, 1964. A tramp teaches an old woman how to make a delicious soup starting with a nail.

Preparation time
Story and props: 15–20 min.
Optional Activities
   Make a Pot of Stone Soup: 5–10 min.

Make a Pot of Stone Soup

What ingredients would you need to make a pot of stone soup?

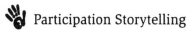

What Do You Do with a Kangaroo?

by Mercer Mayer

Macmillan, 1973

Summary: In this rhythmic tale, a fierce little girl deals with a kangaroo in her bed, a raccoon eating her cereal, a llama wearing her pants, and other bothersome creatures.

Procedure: As the children sit down, give a different puppet figure to seven children in the front row. Explain that they are going to help you with the story and that when you call the name of their characters, they are to stand up next to you. As you read the story, the children will pick up the rhythm, and by the time you reach the third animal, they are ready to answer the question, "What do you do...?" As you eliminate each character, have the child with that character move to your right and stand in a line.

When you get to the last question on what to do about all the animals, pause for a moment and ask what the children would do. After hearing a few of their solutions, finish the story with an upbeat final tone.

Materials needed:
- paper plates
- markers
- craft sticks
- masking tape

You need seven puppets for the story: a kangaroo, an opossum, a llama, a raccoon, a moose, a tiger, and a camel. Trace the animals onto the paper plates. Color or paint the animals. Tape the craft sticks at the bottom of the plate to use as holders.

Optional Activity

Animal Puppets

Give each child a paper plate and craft sticks. Each child should draw an animal on the plate, color the animal, and attach craft sticks as handles on the bottom of the paper plate.

Materials needed:
- paper plates
- markers, crayons, or paint
- craft sticks
- masking tape

Related Books: Devilish Imps

Gantos, Jack. *Rotten Ralph.* Boston: Houghton Mifflin, 1976. Rotten Ralph, the nastiest cat around, is reformed under most unusual circumstances.

Lobel, Arnold. *Prince Bertram the Bad.* New York: Harper, 1963. Mischievous Prince Bertram finds himself changed into a dragon by a witch.

O'Keefe, Susan Heyboer. *One Hungry Monster: A Counting Book in Rhyme.* Illustrated by Lynn Munsinger. Boston: Joy Street, 1989. A group of naughty monsters make so many demands to be fed that a small boy finally orders the monsters out of his house.

Sendak, Maurice. *Where the Wild Things Are.* New York: Harper, 1963. Without his supper, unruly Max is sent to bed, where he goes off into the land of the wild things.

Giveaway: "What Would You Do About a Kangaroo?" (activity sheet)

 Preparation time
Story and puppets: 30–40 min.
Optional Activities
   Animal puppets: 15–25 min.

What Would You Do About a Kangaroo?

Find the pictures in the key below and place the letter in the blank spot under the picture. The answer will tell you what to do with a kangaroo.

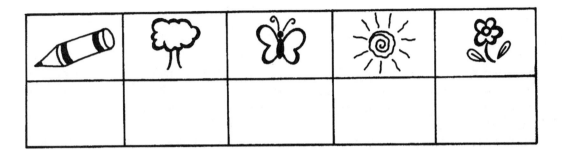

# *Puppetry*

Puppetry is an art form that has endured for years. When given life through the imagination, any inanimate object can become a puppet. The object can be as complicated as a string marionette or as simple as a finger shadow puppet. Puppets are always a hit with children, bringing gleams to their eyes and providing great enthusiasm.

Puppetry has been a major theatrical practice in many areas of the world for centuries. It was a vital part of the religious rituals of ancient Greece and Rome and flourished in ancient Egyptian society. Throughout Europe, famous puppet troupes traveled across the continent entertaining children and adults alike. In Salzburg, Austria, a permanent puppet theater presents entire operas through marionettes, and in Russia, Hungary, Czechoslovakia, and Poland, there are still well-financed puppet companies.

From the beginning, puppet shows were very popular and quickly became a favorite amusement for all classes of society. At first, the shows were primarily based on familiar stories and legends, but as time passed, the shows became more polished, and the puppets began to acquire the voices of the people. Under the guise of entertainment, the puppets could spread the news, make fun of the pretentious, parody current events and living people, and air current abuses in government and society.

During the sixteenth century, the puppet Punch was introduced to the English by Italian and French puppeteers. Although Punch was originally used as a marionette with more bark than bite, as he became more popular in England, he assumed a purely British character. English puppeteers used the hand puppet medium so that Punch would be able to pick up things and throw them around more easily.

In the Far East, puppets are used to perform classic dramas in theaters, in temple courtyards, and on street corners. These traditional puppet shows usually portray good and evil characters locked in combat with one another. Perhaps the most renowned puppets in Japan are the Banraku puppets, which date back over three centuries. The four-foot-high Banraku puppets are so complex that they require three operators to manipulate their movements while the narrator tells the story and speaks the dialogue.

In India, string and shadow puppets are used to tell the adventures of heroes, gods, and demons in the form of shadow and two-stringed marionettes. The Tholumatta shadow puppets are approximately four to five feet high and are made of leather from animals that died naturally rather than from slaughtered animals.

It would be impossible to discuss the history of puppetry without mentioning the Chinese. Chinese hand puppets are known for being small and very delicate. Chinese shadow puppets are noted for their exquisite lines and beautiful colors, achieved by carefully staining hides. Rather than being operated from the bottom like most shadow puppets, they are operated by a rod attached at the neck. The puppet plays are used to relate the history and folklore of the people rather than to present religion-oriented scripts as do the Hindu puppet plays.

The main differences between European and Oriental puppet shows are the temperament and point of view presented through the puppets. Oriental puppets are shy and gentle and rarely perform practical jokes on others. European puppets tend to be rather sarcastic, grotesque, realistic, and very practical.

Puppeteers in the United States have borrowed many ideas and traditions from other cultures and in the process have created many new puppet traditions. In the early 1940s, Edgar Bergen and his rod puppet Charlie McCarthy were so popular that they had their own radio show. Later, in the early days of children's television, Fran Allison used the puppets Kukla and Ollie to entertain children throughout the nation. The baby boom generation of the 1950s and 1960s were entertained by the marionette Howdy Doody as well as by Shari Lewis and her simple cloth hand puppets Lamb Chop and Hush Puppy. Fred Rogers from *Mr. Roger's Neighborhood* offers an entire make-believe land populated by a number of hand puppets. Jim Henson's Muppets of *Sesame Street* fame are perhaps the most well-known puppets on children's programs today. The Muppets' success has led to the recognition of puppetry as a legitimate means of educating children. Today, many educational and theatrical films feature puppets in starring roles, and there is increased use of puppets in schools, libraries, homes, and even the business community as tools for entertainment and education.

Puppets can be an important part of any storytelling session. By using a simple hand puppet at the beginning of a story session, the storyteller can quiet a group of children and indicate that the time is special. Puppets are good icebreakers and can be used to lessen shyness; even the shyest child will talk to a puppet. Puppets provide fun and excitement and create a strong impression on children. They are magnets that draw a positive response in even the most negative child. When presented in connection with the library, a puppet can serve as a mascot or symbol and thus be used to create a community spirit and to provide some good public relations for the library. Undoubtedly, puppetry can be used to enrich children's programs in the library, classroom, and home.

Puppets can be used for a number of purposes, including all of the following:

- *To introduce concepts*—Puppets are very effective when introducing new concepts such as numbers, vocabulary, sounds, and sequencing to children. You only need to watch *Sesame Street* to see how the Muppets are used to introduce number and letter concepts to preschoolers. Using puppets can increase the tactile, visual, and auditory skills of children. They hear the words as spoken through the puppets and see the message in the puppets' actions.

- *To reinforce self images and to serve as an icebreaker*—When a new child enters a group in a classroom, story session, or any other new environment, it is often a threatening situation for even the most self-confident individual. By using a puppet to ask the child questions as a means of introduction, you take away the threatening environment and provide a more pleasurable experience

for all. Puppets are good icebreakers and means of relieving tension.

- *To build awareness of other cultures*—By using puppets, you can more easily introduce different cultures to children. A puppet dressed in a costume from another country can be used to tell children about the country in a enjoyable manner. And, such a presentation will help the children to retain the information.

- *To tell stories*—Librarians and teachers have used puppets for years to relate stories to children. Puppetry is a natural extension to the art of storytelling. The puppet is an accessory that introduces an element of the theater—a step away from reality where anything can happen. The use of puppets can enhance the skills of a storyteller. Stories come to life in the persona of the puppet.

Here are some examples of different ways to use puppets with your storytelling.

1. A puppet can be used to introduce a story, to help read it aloud, to ask questions occasionally, and to show the pictures to the audience.

2. A puppet of the main character from the story can be used as a focal point. Some examples of lead puppets include Curious George, Amelia Bedelia, Max, and Rotten Ralph.

3. The storyteller can use a cast of characters to reveal the story. A good example of this method would be to tell *Goldilocks and the Three Bears* using a series of four hand puppets.

4. Puppets can be used in a purely theatrical approach. As the storyteller reads or tells the story, the children use puppets to act out or pantomime the action in the plot.

- *To entertain*—Perhaps the most important use of puppets is purely to entertain. Not only are the puppets entertaining for the listeners but they are also entertaining for the puppeteers. Puppets are a guaranteed attention getter and can be used in all sorts of situations. Puppet shows are magic for everyone involved.

When using puppets as an integral part of story-telling, there are three main points, or steps, to keep in mind.

The first step is to choose a story for dramatization. The key to any good puppet show is a good script. The script can consist of a procedure as simple as reading from a storybook while the puppets move to the action or as complex as writing an adapted version of a story to use with puppets.

Any story can be readily adapted to use with puppets, but some stories are more easily adaptable than others. It is best to choose a story with a strong, simple action line; only a few main characters; and limited props and visuals. And, it is essential that the storyteller enjoys the story. Folktales and children's classics such as *Henny Penny* and *The Three Billy Goats Gruff* are old standbys.

The second step is to decide on the type of puppets to use with the story. Choose the type that will best represent the book characters. Easy puppets such as stick puppets are best used with impromptu performances while interest in the story is at its peak. More complex puppets such as marionettes take a great deal of time to construct but can be used for numerous performances.

The third step is to produce the puppets and the show; it includes such tasks as acquiring materials, producing puppets and sets, and arranging staging (formal or informal theater), and lighting. Avoid stories that have a large number of props, visuals, and characters.

Types of Puppets

All types of puppets require time, effort, and thought to create and to use. There are many varieties of puppets that you can create, but all fall into one of two major categories—hand or marionette.

If you are interested in using puppets as an integral part of your storytelling sessions, start collecting materials that might be useful in making and creating puppets. Following is a list of some of the types of materials that are useful for puppet makers.

Puppet Body

socks	boxes	shirt cardboard
paper bags	rubber balls	Styrofoam balls
felt	clothespins	wooden spoons

plastic bottles	egg cartons	corks
tissue paper rolls	sponges	paper scraps
tissue paper	clay	balloons
paper plates/cups	gloves	mittens
papier-mâché strips		

sticks (tongue depressors, craft, dowel, Popsicle, and even chopsticks)

Heads for Hand Puppets

Styrofoam eggs	potatoes	light bulbs
dish scrubbers	apples	modeling clay
play dough	doll heads	balls of yarn
old stuffed animals		

(Heads for puppets can be created out of almost anything.)

Puppet Trimmings

wallpaper scraps	fabric scraps	carpet scraps
yarn	pipe cleaners	lace
beads	cotton fiber	cotton
straws	feathers	buttons
rickrack	thread	sequins
pasta	cotton	ribbon
pom-poms	tassels	paper doilies
braided trims	fur scraps	iron-on tape
spools	scouring pads	seeds

Other Supplies

construction paper	glue	scissors
felt-tipped pens	netting	newspapers
tracing paper	crayons	Velcro
paintbrushes	string	nails
paint	wire	screws
paper fasteners	rubber bands	masking tape
pins	needle & thread	

When creating puppets you are limited only by your imagination. Be creative and add your own personal touches.

Hand Puppets

Although there are only two main types of puppets, there are variations within the two categories. Hand puppets are manipulated without strings by the puppeteer's hand or a part of the hand. They are useful in speaking dialogue because the head of the puppet captures the listener's attention and makes the story more realistic. Some of the different types of hand puppets are discussed on the following pages.

Finger Puppets

A finger puppet is any puppet that fits on one or more fingers and can be easily manipulated by the puppeteer. These puppets are portable and can fit in a pocket and be displayed at will. Finger puppets are a natural way to introduce simple, uncomplicated rhymes, poetry, and stories to very young children. They are best used with small groups of children or in a one-on-one situation. Commercial sets of finger puppets are available from or in a number of sources, including school supply outlets, coloring books, and paper doll sections of stores. You can easily create your own finger puppets. The following are some of the basic variations of finger puppets:

Thumb puppets—Use washable felt-tipped pens to draw a character's features on your thumb. Fingers are good too!

Tissue paper roll puppets—Cut a tissue tube to fit two to three fingers. Cover the fingers with construction paper, and use felt-tipped markers to draw the facial features on the tube.

Glove finger puppets—Cut fingers from an old pair of gloves. Decorate the fingers with yarn, eyes, etc., to create a personality for the puppet.

Paper finger puppets—Cut strips of paper to fit around the finger. Decorate the face for the puppet using purchased eyes, crayons, markers, etc. An alternative type of paper finger puppet involves drawing a character on paper that is approximately three to four inches long, leaving space at the bottom for two finger-size holes. Decorate your hand-drawn character using yarn, wiggle eyes, buttons, etc., to add more features. Cut two holes for your fingers to fit through to manipulate the puppet. You can also cut out characters from a coloring book, catalog, or magazine and use them for puppets. Cut paper to go around your finger and glue the paper to the back of the puppet. Use this loop to manipulate the puppet.

Paper cup puppets—Cut two holes in the bottom of a small paper cup to use to control the puppet. Decorate the top of the cup with buttons for eyes and drawn on facial features. Glue on paper ears and yarn hair.

Fist Puppets

Fist puppets involve the use of the entire hand including palm and fingers to manipulate. They can be made from any number of materials. There are two main types of fist puppets—those with moving mouths and those with moving bodies. The traditional homemade fist puppet is probably the most effective with groups of children. However, it is possible to purchase some well-made commercial fist puppets. They are usually of the sock, glove, and felt type and are available in school supply stores, craft shops, gift shops and department stores. One word of caution—you may find that commercial puppets are available in limited varieties and will not always fit your specific needs. You can make your own fist puppets using a variety of methods, including the following:

Sock puppets—Perhaps the most popular fist puppet and the easiest to make is the sock puppet. Sew felt ears and buttons for a mouth on an old sock, and glue on eyes for a homemade puppet. Use your hand to control the mouth.

Whole-hand puppets—Create a puppet character by using washable pens to draw the features on your hand.

Fabric or felt puppets—These puppets are useful for very simple characters such as animals. Draw the simple body form of a character such as a rabbit on a piece of paper. Cut two copies of the form from fabric or felt. Sew the two pieces together leaving the bottom open to insert into the puppeteer's hand. Decorate the character. Another method of creating this type of puppet is to cut a body form from material and to sew it together leaving an opening at the top and one at the bottom. Attach a foam head to the body by inserting a tube into the foam ball and using the tube to control the head while the fingers control the bottom of the puppet.

Paper bag puppets—To create a paper bag puppet, use either a stuffed or a flat brown paper bag. For flat puppets, draw or paint faces on the folded end of the closed paper bag. Draw the upper lip on the top part of the fold and the lower lip on the bag itself. For a stuffed puppet, stuff the paper bag with newspapers, insert a dowel rod or stick in the open end of the bag, and tie the bag shut around the stick. Decorate the puppet. Paper bag puppets are especially effective as fairy tale characters, holiday characters, community helpers, and farm and zoo animals.

Box puppets—Any type of box can be used, but the small individual cereal, gelatin, and pudding box sizes are especially effective for this type of puppet. Use tape or staples to attach two boxes together at the open end. By inserting a hand in each box, you can make the puppet talk and move. Cover the boxes with paper, fabric, or paint. Paint or draw faces on the closed ends of the boxes. Add other facial features using materials such as fabric, pipe cleaners, and yarn.

Nylon stocking puppets—These puppets are especially good for snake and dragon characters. At one end, stuff an old nylon stocking with cut-up bits of other old nylons. Decorate the puppet to resemble a snake or a dragon, and use the open end of the stocking for the puppeteer to control the movements.

Sandwich bag puppets—Cut two holes on each side of a sandwich bag, one for the thumb to fit through and one for a finger. Cut a hole in the center for a nose. Decorate the puppet with such things as markers, glued on paper features, and yarn.

Footie puppets—Decorate the bottom of an old footie, and use it as a hand puppet.

Mirror puppets—Glue a construction paper face and features to the back of an old hand mirror to create a hand puppet.

Vegetable or fruit puppets—Wash any type of vegetable or fruit and decorate it to create a temporary but effective puppet. Potatoes, carrots, apples, peppers, and tomatoes are examples of vegetables you can use.

Mitten puppets—Cut two holes on the sides of the mitten for the arms (your fingers). Decorate the puppet and use it as you would a glove or sock puppet.

Glove hand puppets—Although glove puppets are a type of finger puppet, they are hand puppets. You can use the entire glove with each finger representing a character in the story. This method is especially useful with stories such as *Goldilocks and the Three Bears*, *The Three Little Pigs*, and *The Three Billy Goats Gruff*. You can use a finger for each of the three pigs and the wolf and still have a thumb left over.

Papier-mâché puppets—As with the fabric or felt puppets, you create bodies for the puppets from two body forms sewn together. The papier-mâché is used to create a head for the puppet. Strips of papier-mâché are draped over a balloon, a clay form, a light bulb, cardboard, or a ball of newspapers. As the papier-mâché dries and you add more strips, the facial features are shaped from it. One advantage to this method is that you are able to create a sophisticated puppet head that closely resembles a story character. Because papier-mâché is very soft and pliable when it is moist, it is easy to mold and to shape the character's head and features.

Stuffed animal puppets—Stuffed animals are a ready-made source to use with storytelling. One way to use a stuffed animal is to split the back seam, remove all the body stuffing, and then use your hand to manipulate the animal. An even easier way to use a stuffed animal is to leave it alone and use the animal as a ready-made puppet. You can make it walk, talk, and move by manipulating the animal's legs and arms. Stuffed animal puppets are very good to use with stories that have a lot of sounds such as *Farmer Duck* by Martin Waddell or *One Windy Wednesday* by Phyllis Root.

Stick Puppets

Stick (or rod) puppets are one of the easiest types of hand puppets for the beginner to create. They are simply puppets attached to a stick or a rod and held by the puppeteer. Stick puppets have several advantages. They can be made in any size and can be adapted for both large and small groups. If you use very large stick puppets, everyone in the audience will be able to see the puppets. Because stick puppets are operated from below, the weight of the puppets is easier to support than is that of marionettes.

However, the use of stick puppets limits the characters' expressions in action and emotion. The storyteller must convey feelings and meaning through voice tone and expression. Stick puppets are especially effective with stories that have a strong and clearly defined action sequence such as that in *Swimmy*, and *What Can You Do with a Kangaroo?* They are also good for stories, such as *Millions of Cats*, which involve a large cast of characters where the children can work on the puppet show presentation as a unit rather than as individuals.

Stick puppets, created from many types of materials, include the following types:

Paper plate puppets—To design a paper plate puppet, you need a paper plate, a stick, and lots of imagination. Draw the character on the center of the plate. Decorate the character by coloring it; cutting out and attaching pictures from a magazine; or using paper, yarn, fabric, etc. Attach a craft stick or dowel rod to the back of the plate, and you have an instant puppet.

Broom puppets—Turn a broom upside down. Cover the bristles with paper, and decorate the paper with a face and yarn hair. The broom handle is your stick. In about 10 minutes, you have a large stick puppet.

Dust mop puppets—These puppets are just like broom puppets except that they have instant hair (the mop strands). Glue felt features on the dust mop to give your puppet personality.

Pencil puppets—Use cotton or tissues to form a head for your pencil puppet. Cover the body with cloth or tissue. Decorate the face to give your pencil personality.

Craft stick or straw puppets—Glue construction paper features to your straw puppets. Add paper arms, ears, etc. For craft sticks you may wish to use felt-tipped pens to draw on the facial features.

Kitchen tool puppets—Any type of kitchen tool will do for this puppet (for example, a wooden spoon, scouring pad, spatula, or whisk). Decorate the kitchen tool with food items such as pasta, nuts, and seeds to give it character. Use paper towel strips as hair.

Sponge puppets—Cut a hole in the sponge to insert a craft stick or dowel rod for the puppet. Glue eyes, ears, mouth, and hair onto sponge to make facial features.

Clothespin puppets—Although spring-type clothespins can be used, the clip clothespins are better for small stick puppets. Draw features on the top of the clothespin, using felt-tipped markers or paint. Use yarn or thread to add hair and construction paper to create arms.

Cork puppets—Glue a small cork to the end of a spring-type clothespin, dowel rod, or craft stick. Add features by gluing felt and paper scraps to the cork.

Shadow Puppets

Shadow puppets are a type of hand puppet that are inexpensive and easy to make and manipulate. The only materials that you need are cut-out puppets, a screen, and a strong light. A shadow puppet is not seen directly by the audience, but instead appears in silhouette or on a screen. The light from behind the puppeteer casts a shadow on the screen or wall. Most shadow puppetry requires minimal effort, skill in manipulation, and in instruction. The key to a good shadow puppet play is carefully planning the scenes and the action. Shadow puppets are especially effective with cumulative tales, where there is a simple repetitive plot line. *I Know an Old Lady Who Swallowed a Fly* and *The House that Jack Built* are good examples of such tales. Stories such as *The Gingerbread Man*, in which a series of characters move across the screen, also make good shadow puppet plays.

One type of shadow puppet is simple finger movement, using lights and shadows on a wall. Another type of shadow play uses simple outlines of objects and characters made out of stiff paper or hand puppets. Stick puppets are excellent to use with an overhead projector to create a shadow play. Shadow puppets can be controlled from under the stage by using cardboard or a stick. Threads, wires, rods, or cardboard strips can be used to make parts of the puppet move. Settings or backdrops for the puppets can be removable or fixed permanently to screens so that they can be changed in a frame stage. One disadvantage of shadow puppets is that, because they are flat, they cannot turn without shrinking in the eyes of the audience. Shadow puppets must exit on the end of the screen opposite the one on which they entered or move backwards.

Masks and Body Puppets

Masks and body puppets are extremely popular with children, especially children of preschool age. Although technically they require more than just the hand to manipulate, mask and body puppets are considered a class of the hand puppet category. Body puppets are a natural transition between puppetry and creative dramatics. Ancient cultures of, for example, the Native Americans, Africans, and Greeks used masks in their theatrical productions. To create your masks or body puppets, try the following ideas:

Paper plate masks—Although this type of mask is not a body puppet, it is effective with young children. Attach hair, ears, a nose, and other facial features to a paper plate. Punch a hole on each side of the paper plate, and attach an elastic string to the back of the puppet so that the mask may be placed over the child's face.

Bag masks—Use large brown paper bags to create bag masks. Cut out spaces for eyes, ears, noses, and mouths. Decorate the bag to resemble the story character. You may choose to use the entire body of the character or simply to shape the bag to make the head of a character such as a lion, bear, or fox.

Cardboard body puppets—Use a large piece of tagboard or poster board for the project. Draw the character on the board. Cut out the face of the character so that the child's face will show through. Then, cut out two holes for the arms of the child. Paint or color the character's body and other features. The child can then become the character by wearing the body puppet.

Marionettes

The second major category of puppets is the marionette, or string puppet. It is perhaps the most popular and most fascinating type of puppet. It is more remotely controlled than any other type of puppet. Marionettes vary in their complexity, and most beginning puppeteers will not want to start with this type of puppet. Because the strings tend to be difficult to manipulate and tend to tangle easily, the use of marionettes requires a good deal of practice. Normally, the marionette hangs at the end of the strings and is manipulated from above. Usually, there are nine strings, with additional strings for special effects that create a wider range of movements.

The traditional multistringed marionettes are complex to make and to operate. Individual bodies, limbs and heads are handcrafted to suit the needed puppet character. A marionette's height can range from 18 to 36 inches. If a marionette is too small, the distinct movements of the puppet are not visible to all of the audience, and if the puppet is too large, the weight becomes unwieldy to operate.

The beginning puppeteers can create some very simple string puppets, including the following two types:

Handkerchief string puppets—Tie a string to a handkerchief or any inanimate object, and use the string to manipulate the object.

Balloon string puppets—Use a blown-up balloon as the body of the puppet. Attach paper faces, tails, ears, and feet to the balloon. Use rubber cement or tape to attach the features. (Paper glue will make the balloon burst.) Attach strings to the head and tail of the puppet, and attach the other end of the string to a cardboard tube or stick to manipulate the action. You can use one or more strings but keep the number small so that the puppet will be easy to control. Instead of balloons, you can use stuffed paper bags or small boxes with strings attached to make simple marionettes.

Presenting Puppet Plays

When presenting a puppet play, consider the size of the audience, the availability of space, and the format for presentation. Keep the format clean and simple so that it will not overwhelm the actual story line.

If you plan to present puppet plays on a regular basis, it might be wise to invest in a commercial puppet theater or to build a permanent one of your own. Commercial puppet theaters can be expensive.

For more informal settings, a number of homemade "theaters" will work for presenting a puppet show, including:

- the top edge of an open book placed on the top of a table or desk used as a miniature stage (a book theater)
- a paper cup with fold-out handles to present simple stick puppets
- a three-sided cardboard theater that opens out on a tabletop (a panel theater)
- an old sheet hung across wires with holes cut in the sheet to view the performance

- an old television set with the insides removed
- a table turned sideways
- a bookcase with the puppeteer on one side and audience on the other
- a large box that is big enough for one or more puppeteers to get inside
- an overturned chair with a sheet, coat, or other material draped across it (This will work if you are in a hurry and nothing else is available.)
- a tablecloth taped or tacked across a doorway
- a windowsill where the audience sits on one side and the puppeteer sits on the other (This is good if there is a window shade to use as a stage curtain.)
- two chairs with a board placed between them and a sheet draped over the board
- a large cardboard carton with a window cut on one side and down the back
- a story apron (A story apron has many pockets where small puppets can be concealed until they are needed in the story. It is especially effective with stories that require an element of surprise.)
- a story tote (Story totes can be used simply as a storage spot or as an integral part of the story. They are used to store props and puppets for the story and can be, for example, a box, bucket, or tote bag.)

Of course, improvisation is always important.

Formal puppet presentations require a great deal of planning and effort. The visual element is important in any type of production including live theater, movies, television, and puppet plays.

In addition to a formal stage or theater, the puppeteer must consider lighting, sound effects, costumes, and scenery and props as well as dialogue to create the desired effect.

Lighting

Lighting is very important in formal puppet shows. Some kind of light is needed for the stage so that the puppets can be seen by the audience. Lighting helps create atmosphere and supplements the scenery, but most importantly, strong lighting allows the audience to see the puppets. The lighting can be as elaborate as you wish, but the strongest light should come from the front to prevent the puppets' eyes from being deeply shadowed. A number of factors should be considered in deciding on lighting, including the intensity of the light (strong lights on the puppets and diffused lighting on the scenery) and colors (bright colors such as yellow and red suggest warmth and happiness, while cool colors such as blue and green suggest distance and more somber situations). Experiment with the lighting to achieve the effect that you wish to convey to the audience.

An ordinary desk lamp will usually work fine as the lighting when it is placed at the top of the theater with the light shining directly on the center of the stage. Other types of lights you might use include:

- night-lights
- flashlights
- penlights
- lamps with the shades removed
- spotlights
- candles
- hurricane lamps

Sound Effects

For formal presentations, the puppeteer can use any number of readily available materials and techniques or actions to produce desired sound effects, including:

- clapping hands
- playing musical instruments
- blowing whistles
- scraping fingernails against sandpaper
- closing or slamming books
- rattling cans
- swirling dried beans or marbles around a pan
- banging spoons, pans, or lids together
- operating fans to create wind

Costumes

Costumes for puppets will vary according to the type of character, time period being portrayed, setting, and available materials. For most hand puppets, the costumes have a simple design and use durable long lasting materials such as cotton, broadcloth, and denim. Most hand puppets involve one basic body material with facial features and simple costumes attached permanently to the body.

Marionette or string puppet costumes are often very elaborate and involve a great deal of time to design and to make. While some of the marionette costumes may be fairly simple, such as a prairie dress and apron, others will involve more complex design and materials such as a ball gown from eighteenth century Paris. Accessories for hand puppets are almost nonexistent while those for marionettes may involve facsimiles of actual shoes, jewelry, hair styles, glasses, etc. from the time period being portrayed. In very complex marionette productions, the puppets may need a series of accessories such as shawls, purses, jewelry, and other items to use during the production.

Scenery and Props

For a permanent backdrop, you can paint the background with light blue or gray, covering all the sides and back of the stage area. Scenery for the puppet presentation can be painted on cloth, cardboard, covered frames, or even window shades that can be raised and lowered as needed. You can also cut pieces of scenery from cardboard and paint and hang them from the back of the theater to give a three-dimensional look to the background. Black velvet makes a good backdrop with simple colored cutout silhouettes used for scenery.

To secure props to the backdrop, you can use magnets, Velcro, or even double-faced tape. Hang stars, snowflakes, cobwebs, bats, and other items by strings or thin wires above the stage if you are using a permanent stage.

Some of the types of props that can be used to enhance a production include throwing confetti across the stage to create a party atmosphere, blowing powder off of a powder puff to make smoke or dust, and using a plant mister bottle to make rain.

The most important thing to remember about scenery and background for a puppet show is to keep it very simple. Too much detail will distract from the action and dialogue. Puppets should stand out from the background not merge with it. The puppets must be able to move freely without hitting each other and knocking pieces of scenery over. Plan the stage setting with sketches before you actually do the puppet show.

"Puppets can be a major catalyst in promoting literature." (Bauer, 1997) Planning, preparing and presenting a story using puppets can be an interesting and imaginative way to hold the attention of the audience and to provide the impetus to a lifetime of enjoying literature. Because they are so popular, puppets are always a welcome addition to any storytime.

Puppetry

The Big Fat Worm

By Nancy Van Laan • Illustrated by Marisabina Russo

Knopf, 1987

Summary: When a big fat bird tries to eat a big fat worm, it sets off an interesting chain of events.

Procedure: This is a cumulative rhythmic story, with only four main characters. Use stick puppets for the characters: a worm, a bird, a cat, and a dog. Attach a cardboard tube to the back of the puppet to use as a holder. Make large-sized faces to represent each of the four characters. As you tell the story, hold up the appropriate puppets. The children will soon pick up the rhythm of the story and say the words with you.

Materials needed:
- lightweight cardboard
- markers or paint
- cardboard tubes or large dowel rods
- tape or glue

Optional Activities

Missing Characters (activity sheet)
Give each child an activity sheet with a picture of a farmhouse and barn on it. The children are to draw in the four missing characters from the story.

Big Fat Bookworm Markers
Using the bookworm pattern, cut out the outline of the worm from a piece of stiff felt. Use markers to add facial features and to decorate the bookworm. If desired, outline the bookworm on the felt before cutting it out.

Materials needed:
- assorted scraps of felt • scissors
- felt-tipped markers

Worm Tracks
Give each child a piece of white paper or cardboard. Tell the children that they are going to cut a worm from string and make tracks on the page, which you can then demonstrate. Dip the string in paint and pull and wiggle it across the page to create worm tracks.

Materials needed:
- white paper or lightweight cardboard

- tempera paint in small jars
- string • scissors

Related Books: More Cumulative Tales

The House that Jack Built. Illustrated by Rodney Peppe. New York: Delacorte, 1970. This tale recounts the old nursery rhyme about all the items involved with building a house.

Hutchins, Pat. *Don't Forget the Bacon.* New York: Greenwillow, 1976. An absentminded child cannot remember the shopping list.

McClintock, Mike. *A Fly Went By.* Illustrated by Fritz Siebel. New York: Random House, 1958. This is the story of a merry chase involving a fly, a cat, a dog, and numerous other animals.

Sierra, Judy. *The House that Drac Built.* Illustrated by Will Hillenbrand. San Diego: Harcourt Brace Jovanovich, 1995. In this cumulative tale, all kinds of creepy characters inhabit the haunted house.

Wood, Audrey. *The Napping House.* Illustrated by Don Wood. San Diego: Harcourt Brace Jovanovich, 1984. One tiny flea creates chaos in the house where everyone is taking a nap.

Giveaway
Bookmarks are always a good storytime giveaways, and for this story, it's even more appropriate to pass out bookworms. For a personal touch, you can outline the bookworms on cross-stitch material, cut them out, and glue onto felt. You can also make the bookworms from perforated paper. For a very inexpensive bookworm, make copies of the pattern on green paper.

 Preparation time
Story and puppets: 20–30 min.
Optional Activities
  Missing Characters: 5–15 min.
  Bookworm Markers: 5–15 min.
  Worm Tracks: 5–15 min.

Missing Characters

Draw in the four missing characters from the story—the big fat worm, the bird, the cat and the dog.

𝒱 *The Storyteller's Cornucopia*

Big Fat Bookworms

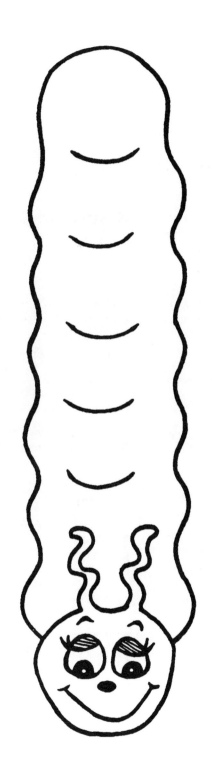

Puppetry

Crictor

by Tomi Ungerer
Harper & Row, 1958

Summary: When Madame Louise Bodot receives a boa constrictor for her birthday, she finds all kinds of uses for her helpful pet. He becomes her companion, and he is a hero to the entire town when he captures a burglar and saves the day.

Procedure: Introduce the story by showing the children the long snake puppet. Tell them that this story is about a special snake who finds a home. As you tell the story, use the props and manipulate the snake puppet into the action of the story.

You may use a stuffed animal snake or make you own puppet. To make a flexible snake, use knit material or nylon hose. Cut the knit material wide enough so that you can sew it together. Turn the snake right-side up and stuff with cotton batting or other materials. You can also make a snake from old nylon hose and stuff it with cut-up pieces of old nylons.

Materials needed:
- long flexible snake from material or nylons
- cotton batting
- needle and thread
- baby bottle (real or doll)

Optional Activities

Baby Boas
Use modeling clay to make small boa constrictors. Let the clay dry, and then use paint or markers to add facial features and other decorations to the boas.

Materials needed:
- modeling clay
- paint and paintbrushes
- markers

Another Adventure for Crictor
Give each child a snake shape cut from construction paper. Explain that each child is to write another adventure for Crictor. An alternative activity is to create a collage picture of Crictor and his new adventure using pictures cut from magazines or drawn by the children.

Materials needed:
- construction paper
- scissors
- glue
- old magazines

Related Books: BOAS!!

Bodsworth, Nan. *A Nice Walk in the Jungle.* New York: Viking Kestrel, 1989. One by one, a boa constrictor eats everyone in Mrs. Jellaby's class.

Kundra, C. Imbior. *To Bathe a Boa.* Minneapolis: Carolrhoda, 1986. A small boy coaxes his reluctant boa constrictor into the bath.

Noble, Trinka Hakes. *The Day Jimmy's Boa Ate the Wash.* Illustrated by Steven Kellogg. New York: Dial, 1980. When Jimmy's pet boa constrictor gets loose on the farm, disaster strikes.

————. *Jimmy's Boa and the Big Splash Birthday.* Illustrated by Steven Kellogg. New York: Dial, 1989. Meggie tells her mother all about Jimmy's birthday party at Sea Land and the unbelievable events that took place.

————. *Jimmy's Boa Bounces Back.* Illustrated by Steven Kellogg. New York: Dial, 1984. A fancy garden party turns into chaos when Jimmy's boa pays a visit.

 Preparation time
Story and puppets: 30–60 min.
Optional Activities
   Baby Boas: 5–10 min.
   Another Adventure for Crictor: 5–15 min.

Puppetry

Helga High Up

By Marjorie Weinman Sharmat • Illustrated by David Neuhaus
Scholastic, 1987

Summary: Helga is too tall even for a giraffe, and her classmates think that she is stuck-up.

Procedure: As you read the story, hold up the appropriate stick or rod puppet.

Materials needed:
- 2 paper plates for each character
- cardboard tube for each puppet (2 for Helga)
- yarn
- construction paper
- scissors
- coloring medium

Only 4 main characters are needed for this story: (1) Helga, the giraffe, (2) Ms. Rabbit, the teacher, (3) Masked Lion, the crook, and (4) Raccoon, the victim. If you like, you may make some of Helga's animal classmates.

Staple two paper plates together, leaving a hole to insert the towel tube to use as a handle. Decorate the faces with paper features for eyes, ears, noses, etc. Use yarn to make hair for the lion, and make a paper mask for the lion. Use two tubes for Helga to promote the image of a too tall giraffe.

Optional Activities

Giraffe Puppets
Give each child a cardboard tube to make a giraffe puppet. Glue yellow paper around the tube or paint the tubes yellow. Paint or color brown spots on the tube. To construct the puppet head, use construction paper that is cut and rolled to fit the tube. Add facial features.

Materials needed:
- cardboard tubes
- paint and paintbrushes or yellow paper
- coloring medium
- scissors
- tape or glue

Giraffe Masks
Students can create masks from paper plates. Cut holes for eyes and noses. Eyebrows, eyelashes, etc., can be made with some coloring medium. Noses and ears can be constructed from paper and taped or glued onto the mask. Use elastic string to attach to the back of the mask.

Materials needed:
- paper plates
- elastic string
- colored paper
- scissors
- glue or tape
- coloring medium
- yarn

Giraffe Growth Charts
This activity is more difficult than the others and is best suited for children ages six to nine. Give each child a long piece of butcher or drawing paper. The paper must be at least twice the height of the child. Let the children draw tall giraffes on the paper and decorate them. When finished, use a tape measure or yardstick to divide the length of the paper into 1" segments. When the children are finished, let them measure themselves against the drawings to see how tall they are. Roll up the charts for the children to take home.

> **Preparation time**
> Story and puppets: 45–60 min.
> Optional Activities
> *Giraffe Puppets:* 25–30 min.
> *Giraffe Masks:* 20–30 min.
> *Giraffe Growth Charts:* 10–25 min.
> *Too Tall Helga:* 5–15 min.

Materials needed:
- roll of butcher or drawing paper
- pencils
- crayons and/or markers
- measuring tapes or yardsticks

Too Tall Helga (activity sheet)

Give each child an activity sheet containing a dot-to-dot picture.

Related Books: Giraffes

Brenner, Barbara. *Mr. Tall and Mr. Small.* Illustrated by Mike Shenon. New York: Henry Holt, 1996, 1994. A giraffe and a mouse are so busy arguing about size that they are almost trapped by a fire.

Collier, Mary Jo and Peter. *The King's Giraffe.* Illustrated by Stephanie Polin. New York: Simon & Schuster, 1996. When the pasha of Egypt sends a giraffe to his friend, the King of France, the people are in awe of the magnificent creature.

Duvoisin, Roger. *Perwinkle.* New York: Knopf, 1976. Perwinkle, the giraffe, and Louis, the frog, learn to listen and to talk with each other.

Rey, H. A. *Cecily G and the Nine Monkeys.* Boston: Houghton Mifflin, 1942. A lonely giraffe and nine monkeys get together for a lively time.

Giveaway

All About Giraffes fact sheet

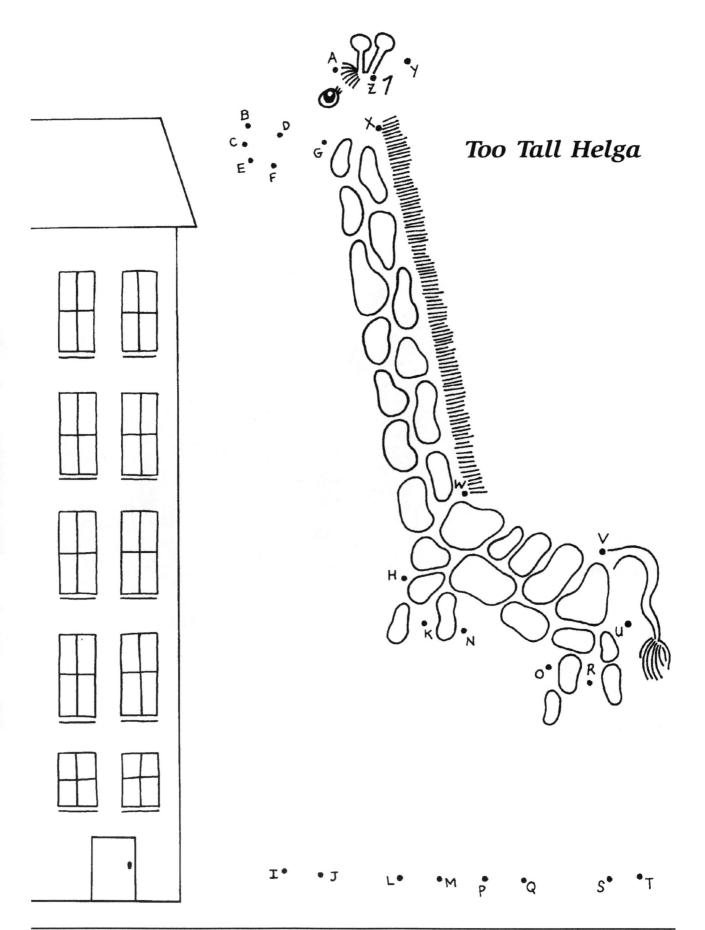

Too Tall Helga

All About Giraffes

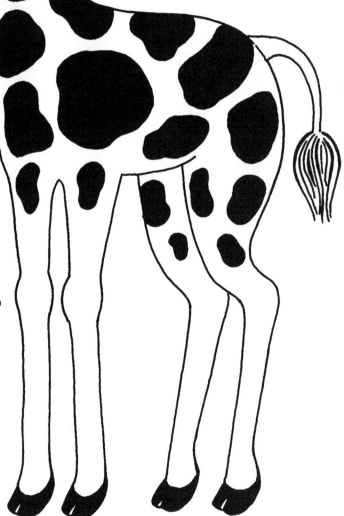

- tongue is 17 inches long
- tail is 3 feet long
- legs of adult giraffes are 6 feet long
- sleeps standing up
- seldom uses its voice but utters a variety of soft sounds
- has patches of tawny (light brownish yellow) to chestnut brown hair

Tallest of all animals

- babies weigh 150 pounds and are 6 feet tall

- eats leaves, twigs, and fruit

- uses its long upper lip & tongue to gather food from tree branches

- live in Africa, south of the Sahara

Puppetry

The Hungry Thing

by Jan Slepian and Ann Seidler
Follett, 1967

Summary: When a Hungry Thing comes to town, no one knows what to feed him until a little boy is able to decipher the Hungry Thing's requests.

Procedure: As you announce the title of the story and begin with the first lines, bring out the Hungry Thing that you have created from papier-mâché. Place a sign around his neck that says FEED ME on the front and THANK YOU on the back. As the story progresses and the Hungry Thing eats, feed him by placing the food items in a hole cut for his mouth. Some of the items can be real, while others will be cardboard facsimiles. At the conclusion of the story, be sure to turn the sign over that is around the Hungry Thing's neck.

Materials needed:

- 2 very large balloons
- flour
- water
- old newspapers
- scissors
- cardboard
- gray latex paint
- coloring medium
- lollipops and cookies
- black paint
- yarn
- masking tape

To make the Hungry Thing, do the following:

Blow two balloons up so they have a 13"–15" diameter and are firm. Tie each with a tight double knot to prevent air from escaping. Use tape to attach the balloons.

To make the papier-mâché, mix equal parts of white flour and water in a bowl. If you need more paste, use the same proportions. Tear or cut newspapers into 1"-wide strips.

Soak the newspaper strips in the flour and water mixture before applying them to the balloons. Crisscross the strips around the balloons until the entire surface is covered. As you apply the second and third layers of papier-mâché, the balloons and the strips will begin to resemble the Hungry Thing. You may need to apply several additional layers, especially on the bottom balloon to complete the creature.

Let the papier-mâché balloons dry for two to three days. After the papier-mâché around the balloons is completely dry, paint it with a gray latex paint, and let it dry for at least twelve hours.

Stretch the end of the balloon and puncture it to allow the air to escape. Retrieve the balloons from the body. Cover the hole on the bottom of the balloon shape with tape so that you will be able to remove the food items. For the top balloon, cut a hole where the mouth should be and retrieve the balloon from there. Add facial features to the Hungry Thing using paint.

Make a large sign to hang around the puppet's neck, the front saying FEED ME and the back saying THANK YOU. Attach a string, and place it around the puppet's neck.

To make the food, use cardboard cutouts of pancakes, pickles, meatloaf, bread, and soup in a bowl. For the other foods, you can use an empty jello box for Jello, a real banana for bananas, real cookies, and real lollipops. You can also cut pieces of beige or yellow yarn into long strips to resemble noodles.

Optional Activity

Sign Makers

Let each child make a FEED ME – THANK YOU sign. Use a small piece of lightweight cardboard for the sign. Punch two holes in the top of the sheet, and attach a piece of string or yarn long enough to go over the child's head. The children can write the words on the signs and decorate them with pictures

Preparation time

Story: 5–15 min.

Puppet: 1–3 hours
(not including drying time)

Optional Activities

Sign Makers: 10–20 min.

of foods mentioned in the story.

Materials needed:
- cardboard
- yarn and/or string
- hole puncher
- coloring medium

Related Books: I'm Hungry!!

Carle, Eric. *The Very Hungry Caterpillar.* New York: Philomel, 1987. A caterpillar eats his way through all kinds of food until he gets a stomachache and has to take a rest.

Fleming, Denise. *Lunch.* New York: Scholastic, 1992 A hungry mouse eats and eats until he has to break for dinnertime.

Gelman, Rita Golden. *The Biggest Sandwich Ever.* Illustrated by Matt Gerberg. New York: Scholastic, 1980. A simple picnic turns into a giant sandwich-building party in this delightful tale.

Reasoner, Charles and Vicky Hardt. *Alphabite! A Funny Feast From A to Z.* Los Angeles: Price Stern Sloan, 1989. Someone is nibbling, gobbling, and chomping his way through an alphabet of goodies.

Slepian, Jan and Ann Seidler. *The Hungry Thing Returns.* Pictures by Richard E. Martin. New York: Scholastic, 1990. Hungry Thing and his daughter return to ask for more outrageous goods such as flamburgers and blownuts to eat.

Giveaway
Lollipops

Puppetry

I Know an Old Lady Who Swallowed a Fly

Retold and illustrated by Nadine Bernard Westcott

Little, Brown, 1980

Summary: A cumulative rhyme about an old lady who swallowed a fly along with a number of other creatures.

Procedure: This edition is just one version of an old cumulative rhyme, "The Old Lady Who Swallowed a Fly." Instead of reading the tale aloud and showing the pictures, use a giant oversized cardboard puppet to tell this tale. As you recite the rhyme and the old lady swallows the animals, place the appropriate creature in her mouth and let her swallow it. Be sure that the last animal, the horse, is too big for the mouth opening. As you recite the last line, pull the oversized puppet sideways so that it will appear to have fallen and died.

Make sure that the puppet is located in a corner so that it does not strike a child when it falls.

Materials needed for Old Lady puppet:
- large brown cardboard box (3–4' high)
- paper
- markers or paint
- paintbrushes
- glue
- red or pink felt
- large grocery bag

To make the oversized cardboard puppet figure, use a large, heavy cardboard box (such as a refrigerator box) as the basic structure. Cut out the outline of the old woman. The figure can be 3' to 4' high. Be sure to cut a large hole for the mouth. You can either cover the brown cardboard with paper or paint the box before adding the clothes and facial features. White works well for the background. Use a pencil to sketch in the outline of the clothes and face and use paint or markers to fill in the details. If you paint the box first, then use paint to fill in the rest of the details. On the back, glue a piece of red or pink felt to cover the mouth opening. Attach a large brown grocery bag to the back of the cardboard puppet to catch the animals as the old lady swallows them.

Materials needed for animals:
- poster board
- markers and/or paint

For the animals that the old lady swallows, you can either use plastic or stuffed animals or make figures from cardboard. To make cardboard creatures, be sure that you start out with a very small fly and increase the size of each animal until you reach the horse, which is too big for the old lady to swallow. Trace the animals onto poster board and use markers to add detailed features of each animal.

You will need a fly, a spider, a bird, a cat, a dog, a goat, a cow, and a horse.

Optional Activities

Old Lady Puppets that Swallow

The children can make swallowing puppets out of paper bags. Use brown paper lunch bags turned upside down. Cut a hole under the fold at the bottom, and place a piece of red or pink felt inside the bag to cover the opening. The children can decorate their old lady puppets and have them swallow all kinds of animals.

Materials needed:
- brown paper lunch bags
- construction paper
- red or pink felt

 Preparation time

Story: 5–15 min.

Puppet for oversized lady: 1–2 hours

Cardboard animals: 45–90 min.

Optional Activities

Old Lady Puppets that Swallow: 15–25 min.

How Many Animals Were Swallowed? 10–15 min.

- scissors
- glue
- crayons and markers

How Many Animals Were Swallowed?
(activity sheet)

Give each child an activity sheet with a picture of an old lady in the center. Surrounding the woman are various animals. The children are to pick out the animals that the old lady swallowed and draw lines from the animals to the old lady's mouth.

Related Books: Swallowing Things

Aliki. ***Keep Your Mouth Closed, Dear.*** New York: Dial, 1966. Poor Charles has a problem of swallowing something whenever he opens his mouth.

Cole, Joanna. ***Golly Gump Swallowed a Fly.*** New York: Crown, 1987. Golly Gump wins a yawning contest and accidentally swallows a number of animals.

Grossman, Bill. ***My Little Sister Ate One Hare.*** New York: Crown, 1996. A Child describes all the things that his sister ate with some disgusting results.

Jackson, Alison. ***I Know an Old Lady Who Swallowed a Pie.*** Pictures by Judith Brown Schachner. New York: Dutton, 1997. When an old lady arrives for Thanksgiving dinner carrying a delicious pie, she decides to eat her offering along with everything else in sight.

Kent, Jack. ***The Fat Cat: A Danish Folktale.*** New York: Parents Magazine Press, 1971. A cat eats everything in sight until he meets a woodcutter with an axe.

How Many Animals Were Swallowed?

Draw a line from the old lady's mouth to each creature that she swallowed.

Puppetry

Inch by Inch

by Leo Lionni
Knopf, 1960

Summary: An inchworm teaches all the birds about measuring and in the process escapes from them.

Procedure: Place the book on a table or just hold it as you use a small finger puppet to present the story to your audience. As you tell the story, use the inchworm puppet to inch across the book or its pages. Afterward, let each child make an inchworm puppet. Tell the children that they can create their own inchworm stories. Also, tell the children that their inchworms are exactly 1 inch long and that they can use the puppet to measure things. Choose several children and let them measure things such as a book, a tile on the floor, the edge of the table, or a leg on a chair.

Materials needed:
- small piece of green felt
- black marker
- scissors
- needle and green thread
- ruler

To make the master puppet, cut a piece of green felt exactly 1" long and wide enough to fit around your finger. You may want to cut a little extra felt to allow for bending your finger. Sew the raw edges of the puppet together and draw eyes and a mouth on it.

Optional Activities

Measuring Inchworms

For the children's puppets, cut the green construction paper into 1" lengths. Have the children fit the puppets to their fingers and tape the puppets together. The children can use a marker or crayon to draw facial features on their puppets.

Materials needed:
- green construction paper
- ruler
- crayons and/or markers
- tape
- scissors

How Big Am I? (activity sheet)

Group the children in pairs. Give each child an activity sheet and a tape measure or a yardstick. Have each child measure his or her partner to see how tall he or she is. The children can then fill in the information on their sheets and take them home.

Materials needed:
- activity sheets
- tape measures or yardsticks
- pencils

Puzzled Worm Rulers

Draw worm shapes on lightweight cardboard. Let the children divide the worm into 1" segments using rulers. Add color to the worm, and cut it into puzzle pieces. Put the puzzles into envelopes for the children to take home.

Materials needed:
- lightweight cardboard
- rulers
- coloring mediums
- scissors

Related Books: Sizes and Measurements

Allen, Jonathan. *Big Owl, Little Towel.* New York: Morrow, 1992. In this small board book, comic illustrations and brief text are used to introduce the concept of size.

Preparation time
Story and puppet: 10–15 min.
Optional Activities
Measuring Inchworms: 5–15 min.
How Big Am I? 5–15 min.
Puzzled Worm Rulers: 5–15 min.

Hoban, Tana. *Is It Larger? Is It Smaller?* New York: Greenwillow, 1985. This wordless book uses photographs to illustrate the concept of large and small.

Kohn, Bernice. *Everything Has a Shape and Everything Has a Size.* Illustrated by Aliki. Englewood Cliffs, NJ: Prentice-Hall, 1966. This book is all about the sizes and shapes of ordinary objects.

Myller, Rolf. *How Big Is a Foot?* New York: Atheneum, 1972. This is a humorous look at different sizes.

Srivastava, Jane Jonas. *Spaces, Shapes and Sizes.* Illustrated by Loretta Lustig. New York: Harper, 1980. The concept of volume is introduced in this easily read book.

Giveaways
Gummy worms

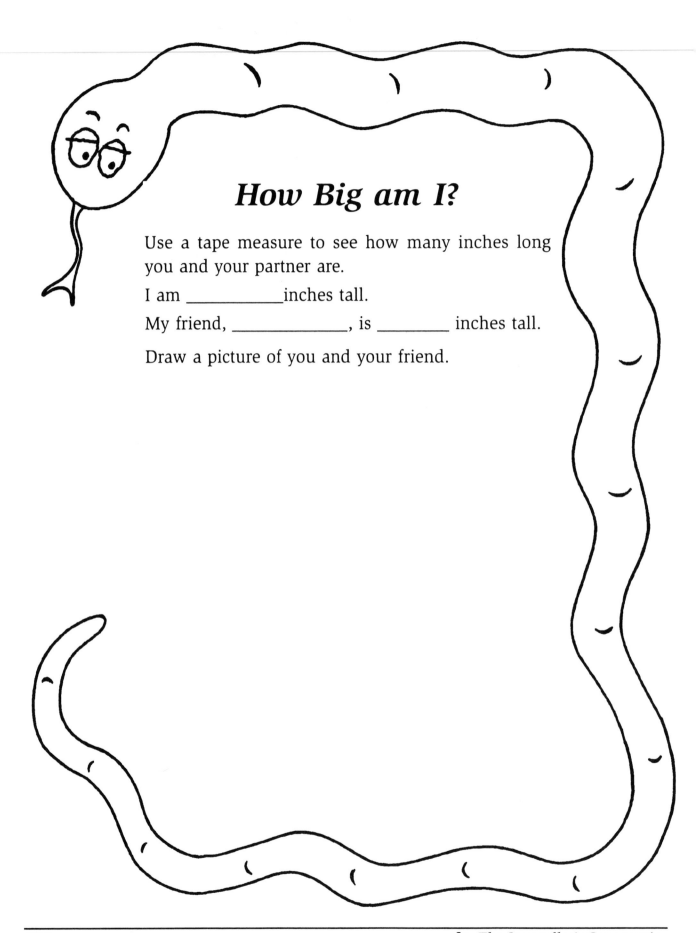

How Big am I?

Use a tape measure to see how many inches long you and your partner are.

I am _____ inches tall.

My friend, _____, is _____ inches tall.

Draw a picture of you and your friend.

The Storyteller's Cornucopia

Puppetry

Katy No-Pocket

By Emmy Payne • Illustrated by H.A. Rey
Houghton Mifflin, 1944

Summary: Katy Kangaroo does not have a pocket like the other mothers, and she tries to find a way to carry her baby Freddy.

Procedure: Use a story apron to hold the puppets for the story. Make an apron like the one in the book, or take a chef or carpenter apron and add enough pockets to hold the puppets. For the puppets, use small stuffed or plastic animals or make your own felt hand puppets.

In the story when Katy asks how other animals carry their babies, pull the appropriate animal from one of the apron pockets. Let the children hold the animals as you continue with the tale.

Materials needed:
- story apron with many pockets
- stuffed or plastic animals or felt hand puppets

You will need figures for Freddy, the baby kangaroo; Leonard the Lion; and Thomas Tortoise. You might want to have a crocodile bird, snail, monkey, skunk, cat, rabbit, raccoon, lizard, squirrel, opossum, frog, and other animals so that more children will have animals to hold.

Optional Activities

Pocket Puppets

Draw an animal face on a sheet of paper, and cut it out. The face should be approximately 2" long. Glue a finger-sized paper ring to the back of the face to complete the pocket puppet.

Materials needed:
- paper
- coloring medium
- scissors
- glue and/or tape

Where Are Katy's Friends? (activity sheet)

Give each child an activity sheet containing a drawing of a pocket. The children are to draw Katy and some of her friends.

Related Books: Pocket Tales

Barrett, Judi. *Peter's Pocket.* Illustrated by Julia Noonan. New York: Atheneum, 1974. Peter likes to collect things in his pockets, so his mother makes him portable pin-on pockets so that he will always have a free pocket in which to store things.

Carter, David A. *What's In My Pocket?* New York: Putnam, 1989. All of the animals have something special to share in their pockets, if you only lift the flap and look.

Freeman, Don. *A Pocket for Corduroy.* New York: Viking, 1978. Corduroy goes off to find a pocket, but he finds himself lost instead.

Katz, Avner. *The Little Pickpocket.* New York: Simon & Schuster, 1996. When his mother's pocket gets too noisy, Joey decides to find a better one and goes exploring in all sorts of interesting pockets.

Rice, Eve. *Peter's Pockets.* Illustrations by Nancy Winslow Parker. New York: Greenwillow, 1989. Peter's new pants do not have pockets, and he has nowhere to put his special treasures, until his mother devises a clever and colorful solution.

Giveaway

"Where are Katy's Friends?" (activity sheet)

Preparation time
Story and puppets: 30 min. (2–4 hours for hand puppets)
Optional Activities
Pocket Puppets: 5–20 min.
Where Are Katy's Friends? 5–15 min.

Ages 3 to 8

Pocket Puppets

Draw an animal face and cut it out. Glue a finger-sized paper ring to the back of the face to complete the pocket puppet.

Example:

Where Are Katy's Friends?

Draw Katy and some of her friends around the pocket.

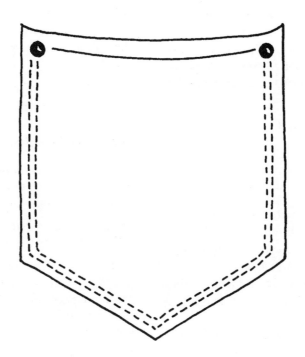

Puppetry

Keep Your Mouth Closed, Dear

By Franz Brandenburg Illustrated by Aliki

Dial, 1966

Summary: Poor Charles the crocodile has a problem. Every time he opens his mouth, he swallows something, and now it is up to Mother and Father to solve the problem.

Procedure: Use a large freestanding cardboard puppet to help with the story. As you tell about Charles and his swallowing problems, use the puppet to demonstrate what happens. As you place the articles in Charles' mouth, be sure that a basket or large grocery bag is behind the puppet to catch everything.

> *Materials needed:*
> - heavy cardboard (approx. 3' high)
> - green and black paint
> - paintbrush
> - box, basket, or brown paper bag

You can use real items or cardboard facsimiles for the articles that Charles swallows. You will need a bar of soap, a wooden spoon, a sponge, Father's hat, a can of baby powder, an alarm clock, a zipper, and a vacuum or any kind of hose. In addition to these items, you will need a brown paper bag and a large sock to place over the jaws.

Draw and cut out a large-sized crocodile figure from the heavy cardboard. Cut the two parts for the jaws separately and attach them with fasteners later. Cut a large hole to insert the materials that Charles swallows. Paint the jaws and body green, and when they dry, add details with the black paint. Attach the jaws so that they cover the hole but are still able to open when necessary. Place a small box or basket under the hole to catch the items. A brown paper bag can be attached beneath the opening to catch materials.

Optional Activities

Close Your Mouth (activity sheet)

Give each child the activity sheet containing an outline of a crocodile. The children are to draw jaws for the crocodile on a separate sheet, cut them out and attach the jaws using fasteners. Add details to the pictures with crayons or markers, etc.

> *Materials needed:*
> - scissors
> - crayons, markers, etc.
> - fasteners

Charles in Clay

Give the children lumps of modeling clay, and let them construct their own versions of Charles and his problems.

> *Materials needed:*
> - modeling clay   •   old newspapers

Related Books: Crocodiles

Dahl, Roald. *Enormous Crocodile.* New York: Knopf, 1978. The enormous crocodile does his best to trap his favorite lunch of juicy little children.

dePaola, Tomie. *Bill and Pete.* New York: Putnam, 1978. Bill is rescued by his toothbrush, Pete.

Dumbleton, Mike. *Dial-a-Croc.* Illustrated by Ann James. New York: Orchard, 1991. Vanessa captures a crocodile in the Australian outback and makes lots of money with him, until the crocodile gets homesick for his country.

Duvoisin, Roger. *The Crocodile in the Tree.* New York: Knopf, 1973. The crocodile hides in a hollow tree until he gets the chance to make new friends.

Waber, Bernard. *Lyle, Lyle the Crocodile.* Boston: Houghton Mifflin, 1965. This title, along with several others, chronicles the adventures of Lyle the friendly and lovable crocodile.

Giveaway

A piece of chocolate cake for each child.

 Preparation time
Story and puppet: 1–3 hours
Optional Activities
    Close Your Mouth: 5–15 min.
    Charles in Clay: 5–20 min.

Close Your Mouth

On a separate sheet of paper, make a pair of jaws for the crocodile below, and attach them using paper fasteners.

Puppetry

Mucky Moose

by Jonathan Allen
Macmillan, 1990

Summary: When the wolf decides to eat Mucky, he encounters some rude surprises and dreadful smells.

Procedure: Begin by asking the children if they can think of words that rhyme with Mucky. "Yucky" will come up and when it does, use the word as a lead-in to this story about a smelly moose.

Materials needed:

- stuffed moose for the puppet
- stick puppet skunks (made from paper cutouts attached to craft sticks)
- clothespin
- gas mask (or any type of face mask)

Optional Activity

No More Smells

Divide the children into groups of two or three. Give each group paper and a sheet of poster board. The children brainstorm and write down five ways to help get rid of the dreadful smells that surround Mucky. Choose one of the methods and use it to illustrate a poster showing how "no more smells" are around Mucky.

Materials needed:

- paper
- pencil
- poster board
- markers or crayons

How Yucky Are You? (activity sheet)

Give each child an activity sheet to use to draw his or her version of how yucky Mucky Moose really was.

Related Books: Mighty Moose

Moskowitz, Stewart. *Too-Loose the Chocolate Moose.* New York: Julian Messner, 1982. All covered in chocolate, Too-Loose can't seem to do anything right until he accidently invents chocolate mousse.

Numeroff, Laura Joffe. *If You Give a Moose a Muffin.* Illustrated by Felicia Bond. New York: Harper, 1991. When a moose eats a muffin, he sets in motion a series of unusual events.

Palatini, Margie. *Moosetache.* Illustrated by Henry Cole. New York: Scholastic, 1997. When his moose-tache keeps getting in his way, Moose devises some creative ways to dispose of the problem.

Waddell, Martin. *What Use Is a Moose?* Illustrated by Arthur Robins. New York: Scholastic, 1997. In order to keep his moose, Jack must find a use for him.

Wiseman, Bernard. *Morris the Moose.* rev. ed. New York: HarperCollins, 1989. Morris tries to convince the other animals that they are moose, just like him.

> ⏰ **Preparation time**
> Story and puppets: 20–45 min.
> Optional Activities
>   *No More Smells:* 10–30 min.
>   *How Yucky Are You?:* 5–15 min.

How Yucky Are You?

Mucky the Moose emitted some very dreadful smells. Draw a picture of your version of Mucky and the yucky smells around him.

Puppetry

Over the Swamp

by Paul Geraghty
Harcourt Brace Jovanovich, 1988

Summary: A hungry mosquito sets off an interesting chain of events in this cumulative tale of life in the swamp.

Procedure: As an introduction to the story, talk about mosquitoes and especially big swamp mosquitoes and their relentless quest for food. Lead into the story by saying that in this story one very hungry mosquito causes all kinds of problems in the swamp.

This is a perfect story to use with clothespin puppets. Use the snap clothespins for the base of the puppet and to attach to the edge of a box, board, or stage to present the story. Copy the characters from the book illustrations. Color the characters with markers, cut out, and attach to a snap clothespin. As you tell the story, snap the clothespin in place along the edge of the stage. As you read the story, the puppets are lined up one after another until the final page when you remove the mosquito puppet from the front of the line and place it at the back of the line.

Materials needed:
- clothespins (preferably the snap type)
- markers
- scissors
- glue
- box, board, or some other device to use to attach the puppets

You will need the following characters: 1) mosquito, 2) dragonfly, 3) frog, 4) fish, 5) heron, 6 snake, 7) crocodile, 8) hunter, and 9) lion.

Optional Activities
Swamp Critter Magnets
Choose one of the characters from the story or another creature of the swamp for this project. Use a large craft stick as the base of the magnet. Draw details on the stick for the critter and attach legs, arms, fur, and other parts as needed. Attach a small magnet to the back of the stick to complete the project.

Materials needed:
- large craft sticks
- glue

- paint
- paint brushes
- wiggle eyes
- fabric, fur, & felt scraps
- small magnets with adhesive on one side
- markers
- scissors
- pipe cleaners

Fat Mosquitoes
Let the children make their versions of hungry fat mosquitoes by using large pom-poms. Use one or more pom-poms for the base of the insect. Glue on wiggle eyes and attach pieces of pipe cleaners for legs. You can use bits of netting or lace for the wings.

Materials needed:
- glue
- wiggle eyes
- large pom-poms
- pipe cleaners
- netting or lace

Related Books: Swamp Life

Bellows, Cathy. *The Royal Raccoon.* New York: Macmillan, 1989. The city raccoon has a little trouble adjusting to life with his country cousins.

Cushman, Doug. *Possum Stew.* New York: Dutton, 1990. Deep in the swamp, Old Possum tries to outwit Bear and Gator.

London, Jonathan. *What Newt Could Do for Turtle.* Cambridge, MA: Candlewick, 1996. Newt gets a chance to repay his friend Turtle when Turtle gets stuck upside down on his shell.

Polacco, Patricia. *Picnic at Mudsock Meadow.* New York: Putnam, 1992. William overcomes his fears and investigates a scary swamp.

Preparation time
Story and puppets: 1–2 hours
Optional Activities
    Swamp Critters: 15–30 min.
    Fat Mosquitoes: 5–15 min.

Puppetry

Petunia

by Roger Duvoisin

Knopf, 1950

Summary: Upon finding a book, Petunia believes she is educated and proceeds to give the other farm animals advice that creates a multitude of problems.

Procedure: Introduce the story by commenting that sometimes knowing part of the facts is not enough. You need to know the whole story as Petunia finds out in this tale. Use paper plate puppets throughout the story to introduce the characters.

After finishing the story have the children suggest other disasters that might have happened to Petunia and her friends when she pretends to read signs and labels.

Materials needed for paper plate characters:
- paper plates
- markers
- scissors
- construction paper
- craft sticks
- yarn
- glue

Cut out facial features from the construction paper and attach them to the paper plate. Attach a craft stick at the bottom of the puppet to use as a handle.

You will need the following characters for this story: (1) Petunia, the goose, (2) King, the rooster, (3) Ida, the hen, (4) Clover, the cow, (5) Noisy, the dog, (6) Straw, the horse, and (7) Cotton, the kitten.

Optional Activities

Barnyard Spool Animals

With this simple craft, a child can create a barnyard animal. You may choose to paint the spools before beginning. The spools will be the bodies of the animals, with small Styrofoam balls used for heads. Glue the heads to the bodies. Glue on moveable eyes. Attach ears, arms, and other features cut from felt, cloth, or construction paper. Use yarn or string for tails and hair.

Materials needed:
- spools
- scissors
- paint
- glue
- yarn or string
- paintbrushes

- small Styrofoam balls
- felt, cloth, or construction paper

Reading Is Fun! (activity sheet)

When Petunia discovers what the inside of the book means, she finds herself in a new world of fun and adventure. Give each child an activity sheet to create a drawing of what he or she looks like when reading.

I Love to Read (activity sheet)

This activity sheet has the names of fifteen types of books. Have children find and circle the words.

Related Books: Farm Life

Azarian, Mary. *A Farmer's Alphabet.* New York: Godine, 1981. Unique woodcut illustrations of things on the farm are shown in this alphabet book.

Bennett, Lee Hopkins, comp. *On the Farm.* Boston: Little, Brown, 1991. Lee Bennett has collected an assortment of poems and rhymes about life on the farm.

Brown, Margaret Wise. *Big Red Barn.* Pictures by Felicia Bond. New York: Harper, 1989. All the farm animals and their babies live in the big barn.

Galdone, Paul. *The Little Red Hen.* New York: Seabury, 1973. A little hen does all the chores while the rest of the lazy animals watch her.

Turner, Gwenda. *Over on the Farm.* New York: Viking, 1993. In this updated version of an old counting rhyme, cows, sheep, mice and sparrows live in the farmyard.

Giveaway

"I Love to Read" (activity sheet)

Preparation time
Story and puppets: 30–60 min.
Optional Activities
Barnyard Spool Animals: 15–30 min.
Reading Is Fun! 5–10 min.
I Love to Read: 5–15 min.

Reading Is Fun!

How do you look when you are reading a story?

I Love to Read

There are many different types of books that you can read. Circle the 15 different types in the puzzle below. You may find the answers across, up, down, or diagonally.

```
T  U  G  E  O  G  R  A  P  H  Y
O  M  R  R  O  M  A  N  C  E  H
P  Y  W  U  Q  S  Y  A  L  X  P
V  S  J  T  M  C  R  T  Y  Z  A
Y  T  O  N  A  I  O  U  L  N  R
S  E  K  E  P  E  T  R  L  O  G
A  R  E  V  O  N  S  E  M  I  O
T  Y  S  D  E  C  I  U  B  T  I
N  O  T  A  T  E  H  X  C  C  B
A  W  E  F  R  N  I  P  X  I  H
F  A  I  R  Y  T  A  L  E  F  P
```

adventure   humor
art   jokes
biography   mystery
fairy tale   nature
fantasy   poetry
fiction   romance
geography   science
history

Puppetry

Picasso the Green Tree Frog

By Amanda Graham • Illustrated by John Siow

Gareth Stevens, 1987

Summary: When Picasso falls into a jar of jellybeans and turns different colors, he longs to be a plain old green frog again.

Procedure: Introduce the story by holding up a puppet of a large green frog and asking the children to guess its name. Although I prefer to use a stuffed animal, it is easy to make a frog hand puppet to use with the story. After the children make a few guesses about the frog's name, tell them that he is Picasso, a green tree frog. Continue by telling the story of Picasso.

If you like, after the story, you can discuss creatures that can change colors or camouflage themselves in their environments.

Material needed:
- green stuffed frog or green frog hand puppet

To make a hand puppet, cut out two outlines of a frog from green felt. With right sides facing, glue or sew the outlines together leaving the bottom open to insert your hand. Turn the puppet right side out. On one side, glue moveable eyes and a felt nose and mouth.

Optional Activity

Cover-up for Picasso (activity sheet)
Give each child an activity sheet with the outline of a frog on it. The children can draw disguises that Picasso might use.

Related Books: Froggie Tales

Dauer, Rosamond. ***Bullfrog Grows Up.*** Illustrated by Byron Barton. New York: Greenwillow, 1976. When a pair of mouse brothers bring a tadpole home, they never think he will outgrow their home.

Freschet, Barbara. ***The Old Bullfrog.*** Illustrated by Roger Duvoisin. New York: Scribner, 1968. An old bullfrog can see all kinds of things, including the heron who is stalking him.

Kalan, Robert. ***Jump, Frog, Jump!*** Illustrated by Byron Barton. New York: Greenwillow, 1981. This is a cumulative tale about a frog who gets away.

Lillegard, Dee. ***Frog's Lunch.*** Illustrated by Jerry Zimmerman. New York: Scholastic, 1994. Frog sits very still on his lilypad waiting for lunch to come by.

Lobel, Arnold. ***Frog and Toad Are Friends.*** New York: Harper and Row, 1970. This is an easy-to-read chapter book about two best friends.

Mayer, Mercer. ***A Boy, a Dog, and a Frog.*** New York: Dial, 1967. This is a wordless tale about three friends.

Giveaway

Jellybeans

 Preparation time
Story: 10–20 min. (If making a hand puppet, add 20–45 min.)
Optional Activities
  Cover-Up for Picasso: 5–10 min.

Cover-up for Picasso

Draw a disguise for Picasso.

Read-Alouds

Some experts say that children should be read to even before birth. The consensus is that parents should also talk, sing, and even recite simple nursery rhymes to their children from birth. They should increase the difficulty and type of reading material as the child grows older. In schools and libraries, reading aloud is an important part of the daily schedule not only in subjects related to the curriculum but also for pure enjoyment.

In many respects, reading aloud is a dramatic performance—a means of creating a mood and interaction between the reader and the listener. There are a number of reasons for reading aloud, including to inform and to explain, to stimulate language development, to inspire imagination, and to arouse interest. However, the most important reason is for pure entertainment and enjoyment. Reading aloud establishes a bond between the listener and the reader.

Selecting a Story

Selecting a picture book, a story, or even a chapter from a book can be a difficult task at times. The following guidelines will help the reader, or storyteller, to choose a story:

- Look for a story that combines action, suspense, and lots of conversation as well as descriptive passages that let the listener absorb the images and mood of the tale.

- Be careful about choosing award winners. Often a book wins an award because of the quality of the writing, but that does not necessarily make the book a good read-aloud.

- Avoid books that many children have seen or heard on television. For example, *How the Grinch Stole Christmas* by Dr. Seuss is a wonderful book, but there are very few children who have not seen this story on television.

- When choosing a picture book, look for a balance between story and illustrations. Choose a book with illustrations large enough to be seen by everyone in the audience.

- Vary the mood and type of material that you choose to read. Do not always read funny stories or dog stories or mysteries. Try to expose the listeners to a variety of different genres of literature.

- Match the readability level of the book to the reading level and interests of the listeners. Occasionally, you may have to edit a book judiciously while reading it. You may have to substitute a new word for one that is inappropriate or offensive to your listeners, to delete or paraphrase sections, or to simplify the story to tighten the action in the story or to provide a more understandable concept. If reading to children of a wide age range, choose something that is more appropriate for the older children.

- Most importantly, choose a story that you like and enjoy reading. Dislike of a book will show in your tone, and the entire experience will be a pointless and unfulfilling event for everyone.

Although reading book chapters aloud is most commonly associated with the classroom teacher, many librarians use this technique to introduce a specific title or theme to children. Chapter reading is especially effective with children in grades 4 to 8. For chapter reading, choose a book that is an attention grabber, that is, one that is full of action or has an unusual twist.

If you plan to use only one chapter as a teaser to stimulate interest, choose a self-sufficient chapter that is complete and leaves the listener wanting to read more of the story. One example might be to read the first chapter from *Sideways Stories from Wayside School* by Louis Sachar. It ends on a suspenseful note and leaves the audience craving "just one more chapter." The same principle holds true for any book that you plan to read to a class over a period of time. Nonetheless, avoid long descriptive passages that are beyond the imagination and understanding of your listeners. For example, you would not read *Dune* by Frank Herbert to a group of fourth graders, but you might use selected passages with a class of tenth graders. If the chapter or excerpt is too long for your time constraints, always stop at a suspenseful point and remember to follow through on reading a chapter or excerpt later. Finish the book unless the audience does not care to listen to it.

The Atmosphere and Setting

Most of the techniques and considerations for reading aloud are common sense things. Attention to the atmosphere and physical setting are as important as the interpretation of the story. For reading aloud in the library, the audience should be seated in a quiet spot away from physical distractions such as windows and people moving around the room. The temperature should be tolerable; too much heat or cold can distract the listeners' attention.

The children should be seated near the reader, with everyone on the same level. Kneeling, sprawling, and leaning tends to lead to a restless audience, so it is best to seat the children in a semicircle with the reader sitting on a chair or stool just slightly above them, thus ensuring that even the children in the back row can see the illustrations in the book.

One of the best methods for reading a picture book aloud is to hold the book to one side at or right below shoulder level. Right-handed people tend to hold the book on the right side, while left-handed people use the left side. You can hold the book with one hand at the bottom of the book and use the other hand to turn the pages. Practice reading and showing the pictures to avoid problems such as holding the book at a slant with the pictures aimed at the ceiling or covering parts of the page with your fingers. Know the story well enough so that you only have to glance at the words occasionally, while maintaining frequent eye contact with the listeners—all of the members of the audience.

Reading Style

Oral reading style is usually developed over a period of time with lots of practice and experience. Some points to consider in developing your own personal reading style are:

Voice Tone and Pitch

Your first goal is to have an understandable delivery.

Careful enunciation and attention to the ends of words and sentences help listeners pay attention to the story and not to the reader's voice. Good breathing techniques support a voice and aid in developing different voice tones. Look up the pronunciation of unfamiliar words before you begin to read.

Volume Control

Controlling the volume of the voice is often difficult for the beginner. Make sure that everyone in the audience can hear you; ask the children in the back row if they can hear you. Of course, there are times when raising or lowering your voice can enhance the story. The experienced reader develops a sense of knowing when and where to pause to heighten the drama and when to lower or raise the pitch to emphasize a point.

Expression

Use plenty of expression in your voice, and change the tone and pitch if the action in the story warrants a change. However, it is not necessary to create special voices for each character or to act out a dramatic scene for every event in the story. A good plot and strong characterization in a book speak for themselves.

Pace

Adjust the pace of the story to fit its style and contents. If you read too slowly, your listeners will fidget and lose track of the plot. If you read too fast, your listeners cannot keep up with the story and savor its contents. Read in a slow even pace so that the children can see the pictures without feeling hurried and can build mental pictures of their own about the characters. During a suspenseful part of a story, you might slow down and draw out your words to prolong the suspense and to bring the listener to the edge of his or her seat, anticipating your every word.

Tips to Enhance the Read-Aloud

You can enhance read-aloud sessions by providing information to the children about the author. Give them a little information and insight into the person behind the story. Add a third dimension to the book whenever possible by using puppets, costumes, etc., that relate to the story. For example, pass out bubble gum to all the children after you read *Bubble*

Gum in the Sky by Louise Everett, have a bowl of blueberries nearby when you read *Blueberries for Sal* by Robert McCloskey, and hold a stuffed "Wild Thing" on your lap when you read *Where the Wild Things Are* by Maurice Sendak. You will find many other enhancement ideas in the discussions of specific stories in this book.

At the end of a read-aloud session, just stop. Leave the interpretations of the book and characters to the listeners. Encourage discussions on books and reading, but do not lecture or analyze the material you read to the children. Let them enjoy the story for no other reason but pure pleasure.

Finally, reading aloud is not intended as a substitute for traditional storytelling, instead it is just one more way to present literature to children and to encourage them to read more.

Suggested Reading

For suggestions on books to read aloud, consult any of the following sources:

Cole, Joanna. *The Read Aloud Treasury*. New York: H. W. Wilson, 1988.

Freeman, Judy. *Books Kids Will Sit Still For: The Complete Read-Aloud Guide.* New York: Bowker, 1990.

———. *More Books Kids Will Sit Still For: A Read-Aloud Guide.* New York: Bowker, 1995.

Kimmel, Margaret Mary, and Elizabeth Segel. *For Reading Out Loud! A Guide to Sharing Books with Children.* rev. ed. New York: Dell, 1991.

MacDonald, Margaret Read. *The Parents Guide to Storytelling.* New York: HarperCollins, 1995.

Trelease, Jim. *The Read-Aloud Handbook.* 4th ed. New York: Penguin, 1995.

Arthur's Tooth

by Marc Brown
Little Brown, 1985

Summary: Arthur tries everything to make his loose tooth fall out so that he will not be the only one in his class with baby teeth.

Procedure: Ask the children if anyone has had a tooth fall out. After listening to the responses, lead into the story by saying that this book is one of a series of stories about Arthur, the aardvark. In this story, Arthur is having trouble with a loose tooth. Proceed to read the story.

Optional Activities

Make a Smile
Have each child draw a large pair of lips on a sheet of paper. Cut out the lips. Add a toothy smile by cutting out and gluing small pieces of paper to the lips.

Materials needed:
- white drawing paper
- scissors
- glue and/or paste
- coloring medium

Where's My Tooth?
Create an activity sheet with drawings of Arthur's animal friends. Each animal is smiling, but none of the characters have teeth. The children should draw teeth for each of the characters.

Related Books: My Tooth

Bate, Lucy. *Little Rabbit's Loose Tooth.* Illustrated by Diane deGroat. New York: Crown, 1975. When Little Rabbit's tooth comes out in her ice cream, she puts it under her pillow for the tooth fairy.

Buller, Jon, and Susan Seade. *No Tooth, No Quarter!* New York: Random House, 1989. When Walter loses his tooth, his chances of getting money for it are slim, and the apprentice tooth fairy assigned to get his tooth is in hot water.

LeSieg, Theo. *The Tooth Book.* New York: Random House, 1981. Rhymes and cartoons tell all about teeth.

Nerlove, Miriam. *Just One Tooth.* New York: McElderry Books/Macmillan, 1989. A wide-eyed bear cub who is dismayed at the loss of her tooth is comforted when the fairy promises that a new one will grow back.

Williams, Barbara. *Albert's Toothache.* Illustrated by Kay Chorao. New York: Dutton, 1974. When Albert, the turtle, complains of a toothache, no one believes him until Grandmother comes to visit and knows how to cure him.

Giveaway
Fact sheet on teeth

 Preparation time
Story: 5–10 min.
Optional Activities
   Make a Smile: 5–15 min.
   Where's My Tooth? 5–10 min.

Some Facts About Teeth

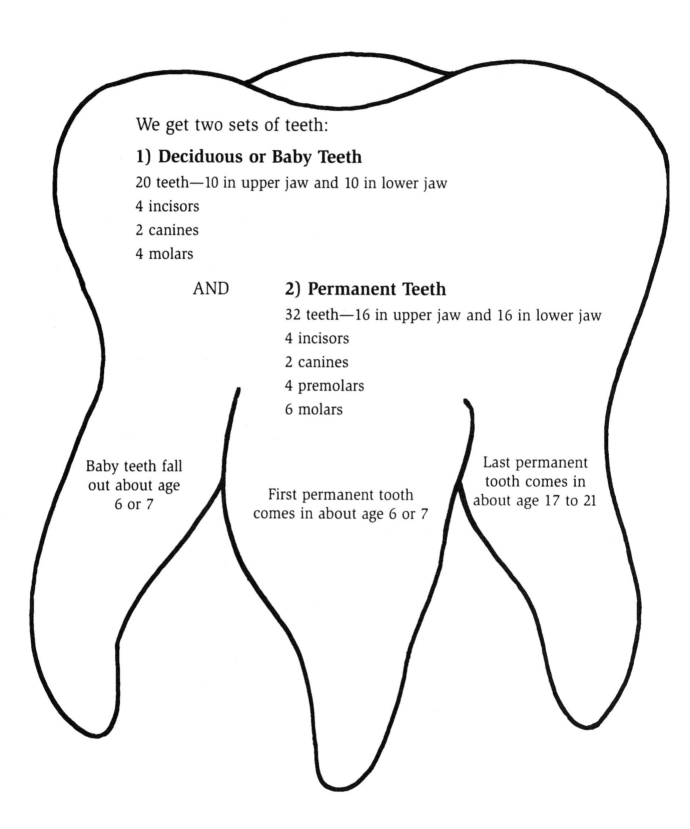

We get two sets of teeth:

1) Deciduous or Baby Teeth

20 teeth—10 in upper jaw and 10 in lower jaw

4 incisors

2 canines

4 molars

AND **2) Permanent Teeth**

32 teeth—16 in upper jaw and 16 in lower jaw

4 incisors

2 canines

4 premolars

6 molars

Baby teeth fall
out about age
6 or 7

First permanent tooth
comes in about age 6 or 7

Last permanent
tooth comes in
about age 17 to 21

A Bad Case of Stripes

by David Shannon
Blue Sky, 1998

Summary: Camilla Cream is so worried about what other people think of her that she breaks out in "a bad case of stripes."

Procedure: Begin the session by asking the children if anyone has ever had a "bad day" when everything seems to go wrong. Discuss a few of the answers you get and then lead into the story by saying, "Camilla Cream woke up one morning with a very bad case of stripes." Proceed to read the story aloud to the group.

Optional Activities

I Woke Up One Day and _____

Write a story about waking up to find that you have _____. Have the children fill in the blank and write an outrageous story about a bad day. Draw illustrations for the cover of the story.

What Happened to Me?

Give each child a long strip of paper cut to match the height of the child. Divide the group into pairs. Have one child place the paper on the floor and lay on top of it. The second child then draws an outline of the body. Reverse jobs so that everyone ends up with an outline of their own body. Draw a self-portrait on the outline and some type of design emulating what happened to Camilla in the story. On the back of the body shape, write a brief story about when, why, and how the bad day happened.

Related Books: What a Bad Day!

Carle, Eric. *The Mixed-Up Chameleon.* New York: Harper, 1984. A very confused chameleon has a tough time until he decides that being just himself is the best.

MacDonald, Amy. *Cousin Ruth's Tooth.* Illustrations by Marjorie Priceman. New York: Houghton Mifflin, 1996. When Cousin Ruth loses her tooth, the whole family is in a dither until the queen solves the problem.

Munsch, Robert. *Purple, Green and Yellow.* Illustrated by Helene Desputeaux. Toronto: Annick, 1992. Brigid loves to draw with markers, but trouble begins the day that she decides to draw on herself with some very special never-to-be-removed markers.

Small, David. *Imogene's Antlers.* New York: Crown, 1985. Imogene is a little girl who doesn't let anything bother her, not even when she wakes up one day with antlers.

Preparation time
Story: 10–20 min.
Optional Activities
  I Woke Up One Day: 10–30 min.
  What Happened to Me? 10–20 min.

The Big Orange Splot

by Daniel Pinkwater

Scholastic, 1972

Summary: When a seagull drops a big orange paint splot on Mr. Plumbean's nice neat house, he decides to turn it into the house of his dreams.

Procedure: Introduce the story by talking about dreams and how many people want to live in a very special house. Mr. Plumbean gets his chance when a big orange paint splot lands on his house. Proceed to read the story. Afterward, have the children make a list of things that are orange.

Optional Activities

Make an Orange Splot Picture

Give each child a sheet of drawing paper and red and yellow tempera paint. Place drops of both colors on the paper. Take a straw and blow through it causing the paint to mix and create a design. Mount the dry pictures on orange construction paper.

> *Materials needed:*
> - drawing paper
> - straws
> - red and yellow tempera paint
> - glue
> - orange construction paper

My Dream House (activity sheet)

Give each child an activity sheet containing a street of identical houses that they can turn into someone's dream house.

Related Books: More than a Home

Burton, Virginia Lee. *The Little House.* Boston: Houghton Mifflin, 1942. A country house becomes surrounded by the city and all its traffic and noise.

Krauss, Ruth. *A Very Special House.* Illustrated by Maurice Sendak. New York: Harper and Row, 1953. This silly story is about an imaginary house.

LeSieg, Theo. *Come Over to My House.* New York: Random House, 1966. A hilarious account of a very special visit.

Shelby, Anne. *Homeplace.* Illustrated by Wendy Anderson Halperin. New York: Orchard, 1995. A grandmother and grandchild trace their family's story in one house from 1810 to the present.

Giveaway

Orange lollipops

 Preparation time
Story: 5–10 min.
Optional Activities
   Make an Orange Splot Picture:
     5–15 min.
   My Dream House: 5–10 min.

My Dream House

Every house on Mr. Plumbean's street looks the same until the day a seagull drops a big orange paint splot on Mr. Plumbean's house. Choose one of the houses above and change it into your dream house.

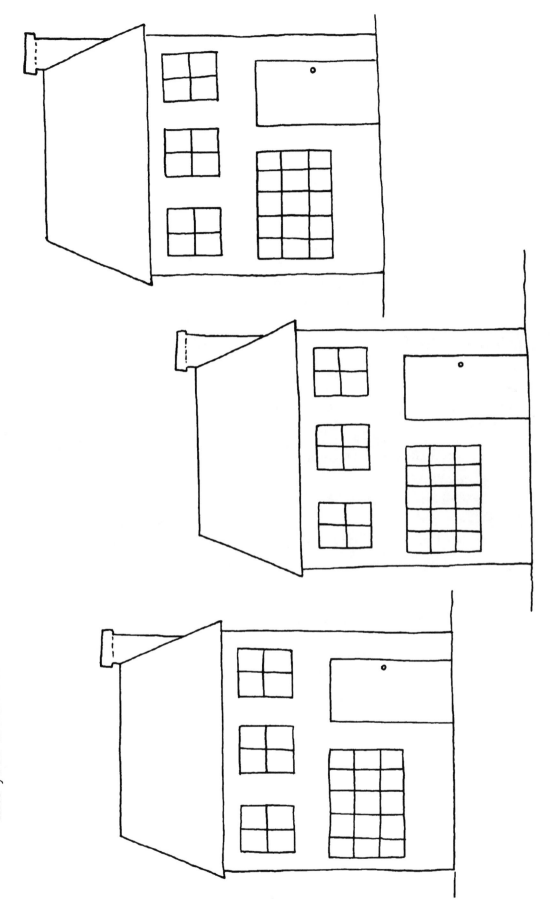

The Biggest Sandwich Ever

By Rita Golden Gelman • Illustrated by Matt Gerberg
Scholastic, 1980

Summary: When a man with a pot happens upon two small children on a picnic, he decides to throw a giant sandwich-building party.

Procedure: Although the illustrations are a little small for large groups, use them as you read this hilarious rhythmic tale. Afterward, have the children help write a recipe for "The _____ Ever." You can fill in the blank with all kinds of things such as "biggest" pie or "best" soup.

Optional Activities

Build Your Own Sandwich (activity sheet)

Have the children create their own giant sandwiches with this activity. The activity sheet has a drawing of two pieces of bread. The children can cut pictures from magazines, use purchased stickers, or draw their own ingredients to create their sandwiches.

Materials needed:
- activity sheets with items drawn on them
- coloring medium
- purchased stickers of food items (optional)
- old magazines (optional)

Sandwich Goodies

If time permits, let the children make sandwiches to eat or to take home. Be sure to have enough bread and a variety of items for the sandwiches, such as peanut butter, jelly, jam, cold cuts, cheese, lettuce, pickles, mayonnaise, mustard, and ketchup.

A Taste of Something Good

Use a bulletin board for this activity. Place drawings of two large pieces of bread with empty space between them together with the heading "A Taste of Something Good." Let each child draw and add ingredients to the sandwich on the board. You can use the bulletin board in connection with a display of cookbooks or stories featuring foods in their titles or scatter book jackets around the bulletin board.

Materials needed:
- drawing paper
- scissors
- coloring medium
- bulletin board

Related Books: Sandwiches

Agnew, Seth M. *The Giant Sandwich*. New York: Doubleday, 1970. When Mr. Magoffin is struck by pangs of hunger, he decides to concoct a giant sandwich.

Benjamin, Alan. *1000 Silly Sandwiches*. New York: Simon & Schuster, 1995. The flip pictures let the reader create all sorts of silly and disgusting sandwiches.

Lord, John Vernon. *The Giant Jam Sandwich*. Boston: Houghton Mifflin, 1972. After a village is bothered by an influx of wasps, its inhabitants build a giant jam sandwich to get rid of them.

MacEwen, Gwendolyn. *Dragon Sandwiches*. Illustrated by Maureen Paxton. Windsor, Ontario: Black Moss, 1987. A whimsical tale of a young boy who takes dragon sandwiches on rye to school for lunch.

Wolcott, Patty. *Tuna Fish Sandwiches*. Reading, MA: Addison-Wesley, 1975. The story is about how a little fish turns into tuna sandwiches.

 Preparation time
Story: 5–10 min.
Optional Activities
Build Your Own Sandwiches:
15–30 min.
Sandwich Goodies: 15–20 min.
A Taste of Something Good:
15–25 min.

Build Your Own Sandwich

What foods would you use to create a giant sandwich?

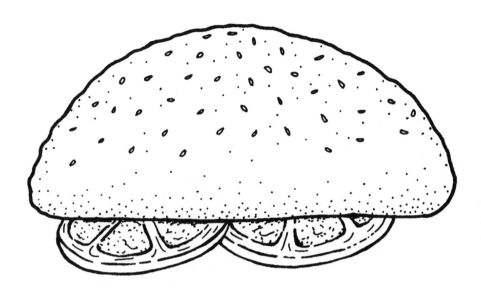

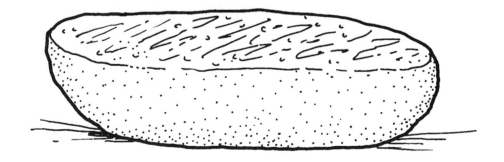

Can I Keep Him?

by Steven Kellogg
Dial, 1971

Summary: Arnold wants a pet, but no matter what he brings home, his mother finds reasons for not keeping it.

Procedure: As an introduction to the story, ask the children the following questions: Does anyone have a pet? What kind is it? Do you take care of it? Give the children some time to tell about their pets. Then, make the transition to your story by saying, "Today, I have a story about Arnold, who wants a pet of his very own." After reading the story, have the children think of other animals that Arnold might have brought home. What objections might his mother have made about them? Tie in this discussion with the activity listed below.

Optional Activities

Strange and Unusual Pets

As a follow-up to the story, cut out pictures of strange and unusual pets as well as regular pets. Mount each picture on a separate sheet of cardboard. Be sure the pictures are large enough for the entire group of children to see. Hold up each picture and have the children think of some reasons why Arnold's mother might not let him have the animal as a pet. You could include pictures of dogs, cats, mice, hamsters, gerbils, snakes, lions, pandas, tigers, elephants, giraffes, alligators, and other exotic creatures.

Materials needed:
- pictures of animals
- glue and/or rubber cement
- cardboard

My Favorite Pet

Have the children draw or find pictures of animals that they would like to have as pets. Mount the pictures on lightweight cardboard, and use them to create a bulletin board or to accompany a display of books on pets and animals.

Materials needed:
- old magazines
- scissors
- glue and/or rubber cement
- lightweight cardboard
- markers, crayons, etc.

Related Books: I Want a Pet

Alexander, Martha. *No Ducks in Our Bathtub.* New York: Dial, 1973. David goes on vacation and returns to find that his 103 fish are really polliwogs.

Balian, Lorna. *The Aminal.* Nashville: Abingdon, 1972. Patrick takes a pet home and has the neighborhood children believing that it is a wild creature.

Chapouton, Anne-Marie. *Ben Finds a Friend.* New York: Putnam, 1986. Ben wants a pet but cannot find one that his parents will accept.

Davies, Andrew and Diana. *Poonam's Pets.* Pictures by Paul Dowling. New York: Viking, 1990. Small quiet Poonam brings six enormous lions to the Special Pet Assembly.

Parish, Peggy. *No More Monsters for Me.* New York: Harper and Row, 1981. Minn finds a baby monster and brings it home to raise.

 Preparation time
Story: 5–15 min.
Optional Activities
Strange & Unusual Pets: 20–30 min.
My Favorite Pet : 10–20 min.

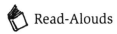

Cloudy with a Chance of Meatballs

By Judi Barrett • Illustrated by Ron Barrett
Atheneum, 1984

Summary: In the town of Chew and Swallow, no one ever has to cook because the food drops from the sky like rain. One day, the falling food overcomes the townspeople, and they must find a way to solve this most unusual problem.

Procedure: Introduce the story by saying that in many households, families have special activities. In this story, Saturday breakfast is special because Grandfather makes pancakes. Ask the group to tell you some of the special times they have at home. Lead into the story by saying that bedtimes are also a special time in the story because Grandfather tells stories to the children. Some of the stories that he tells are a special type called tall tales. Briefly explain that tall tales are stories in which events are greatly exaggerated.

After the story, ask the children to tell you some weather terms, and then have the group incorporate the terms into "Chew and Swallow" weather reports.

Caution: The tongue-in-cheek humor is a little over the heads of preschoolers.

Optional Activity

Weather Reports (activity sheet)
Give the children a list of weather terms, and let them incorporate the terms into nutrition weather reports like those given in the land of "Chew and Swallow."

Related Books: Fancy Foods

Barrett, Judi. *Pickles to Pittsburgh.* Drawn by Ron Barrett. New York: Atheneum, 1997. Kate dreams about the land of Chew and Swallow, where it snows popcorn and rains sandwiches.

Benjamin, Alan. *Ribtickle Town.* New York: Four Winds, 1983. A rhythmic tale of a young boy's dream of a town where houses are teapots and gates are dinner plates.

Koshland, Ellen. *The Magic Lollipop.* New York: Knopf, 1971. Reggie's magic lollipop makes fantastic things happen for him even when all the magic is gone.

Kroll, Steven. *Fat Magic.* Illustrated by Tomie dePaola. New York: Holiday House, 1978. When Prince Timothy finds himself under a fat curse, he must find a way to break the spell.

McGowan, Tom. *Dragon Stew.* Chicago: Follett, 1969. When King Chubby holds a contest to find the most unusual recipe, he never expects a dragon to enter the contest.

Pinkwater, Daniel. *Pickle Creature.* New York: Four Winds, 1979. When Conrad makes a late night trip to the supermarket, he finds a pickle creature and brings it home to take care of.

Rees, Ennis. *Potato Talk.* New York: Pantheon, 1969. This is a silly tale of a man who hears potatoes talking.

Yaffe, Alan. *The Magic Meatballs.* New York: Dial, 1970. When Marvin takes home some magic meat, his family eats it and turns into food.

Giveaways

"Weather Reports" (activity sheet) and list of weather terminology

> **Preparation time**
> Story: 10–15 min.
> Optional Activities
>   *Weather Reports:* 5–15 min.

Weather Reports

Turn these real weather reports into food reports from the town of Chew and Swallow.

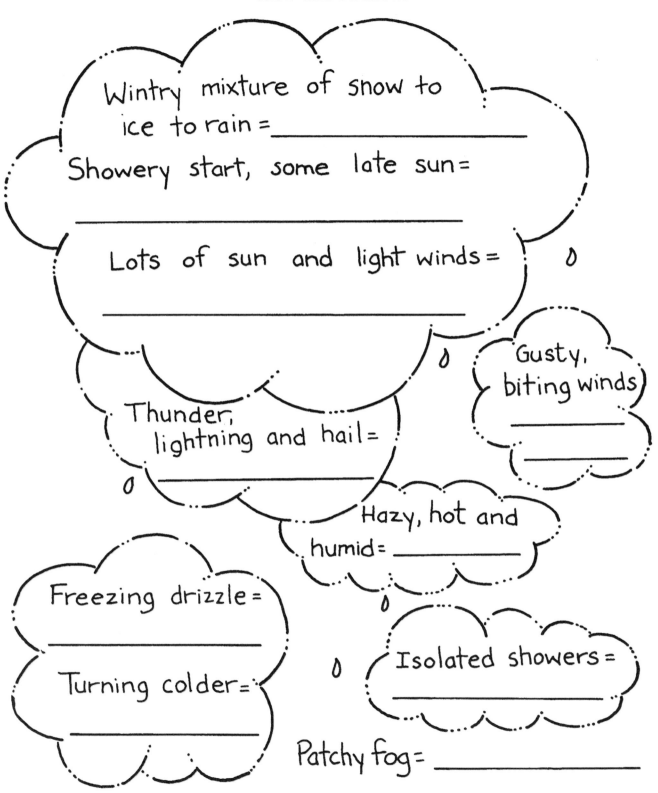

Wintry mixture of snow to ice to rain = _____

Showery start, some late sun = _____

Lots of sun and light winds = _____

Thunder, lightning and hail = _____

Gusty, biting winds _____

Hazy, hot and humid = _____

Freezing drizzle = _____

Turning colder = _____

Isolated showers = _____

Patchy fog = _____

Weather Terminology

developing sun, early cloudiness

diminishing winds

passing flurry

rain likely, ending overnight

sunny with record highs

pleasant and warm

brief periods of showers

a mixed bag, some icing possible

wintry mixture of snow to ice to rain

severe thunderstorm warning

hazy, hot, and humid

showery start, some late sun

cloudy with a few sprinkles possible

variable cloudiness

strong gusty winds

lots of sun and light winds

partly sunny and windy

intervals of clouds/rain

thunder, lightning, and hail

colder air accompanied by flurries

cool, rain spreading eastwards

increasing cloudiness

blustery and very cold

heavy thunderstorms

plenty of sunshine

thunderstorms, clearing late

sleet

arctic air mass

freezing rain

turning colder

funnel clouds sighted

dry spell

flurries possible

slow clearing

springlike

wind gusts of 40 mph

occasional rain

patchy fog

freezing drizzle

partial sunshine

snow squalls

gusty biting winds

fair but cold

becoming windy

breezy and sunny

isolated showers

snow flurries

seasonally warm

sunny, record highs

warm winds

mild and sunny

The Clown's Smile

by Mike Thaler

Harper and Row, 1962

Summary: A clown's smile flits from one person to another in the circus tent while the clown tries to catch it.

Procedure: This book has a very simple story line and requires a one-time read-through to capture its plot and rhythm. It is especially useful for times when you need a short story to fill in some extra time at the end of a formal story hour or when you have a class for only a few minutes. Read the story aloud to the children, showing them the pictures. When you are finished, pass out the activity sheet for them to take home. The activity sheet reinforces the plot of the story.

Optional Activities

Clown Faces

Have the children cut circles, squares, triangles, and other geometric shapes from construction paper. Use the shapes to create a clown face on a sheet of cardboard.

Materials needed:
- construction paper
- scissors
- lightweight cardboard
- glue and/or paste

Clown Figures

The children create clown figures to take home and display. Use plastic or wooden blocks as the body for the clown. Use a small Styrofoam ball for the head. Cut facial features from scraps of felt, cloth, or paper and glue them on the Styrofoam ball. Make a clown hat from paper or felt, and place it on the head. If desired, attach a pom-pom to the top of the hat.

Materials needed:
- plastic or wooden blocks
- small Styrofoam balls
- scraps of felt, cloth, and paper

- pom-poms
- glue and/or paste
- scissors

Give Me a Smile (activity sheet)

The activity sheet is designed for preschoolers through age 6. The children are to give the clown back his smile.

Related Books: At the Circus

Ehlert, Lois. *Circus.* New York: HarperCollins, 1992. Snow cones, bareback riders, and the razzle dazzle of the circus are shown in this bright, colorful book.

Maestro, Betsy, and Guilio Maestro. *Harriet Goes to the Circus.* Illustrated by Guilio Maestro. New York: Crown, 1977. Harriet wants to be first in line to see the circus.

Peet, Bill. *Chester the Worldly Pig.* Boston: Houghton Mifflin, 1965. A pig runs away to the circus and finds himself performing in a cage with five tigers.

Seuss, Dr. *If I Ran the Circus.* New York: Random House, 1956. Morris McGurk imagines what a circus would be like if he owned it.

Vincent, Gabrielle. *Ernest and Celestine at the Circus.* New York: Greenwillow, 1989. Ernest and Celestine go to the circus and find themselves the toast of the big top.

Preparation time

Story: 5–10 min.

Optional Activities

    Clown Faces: 5–15 min.

    Clown Figures: 10–30 min.

    Give Me a Smile: 5–8 min.

Give Me a Smile

Can you put a smile back on the clown's face?

Corduroy

by Don Freeman
Viking, 1968

Summary: Poor Corduroy sits on the department store shelf all alone with a button missing from his overalls until a little girl named Lisa gives him to a home filled with love and friendship.

Procedure: Display a stuffed teddy bear (or a bear hand puppet, if you prefer) as you ask the children if anyone has a favorite toy like the bear that you are holding. Lead into the story by telling the children that today's story is about love and friendship and finding a home.

Optional Activities

Fuzzy Wuzzy Bear

Use with preschoolers to first graders. Teach the children the nursery rhyme "Fuzzy Wuzzy Bear," then use an easy craft activity to reinforce the bear theme. Cut a bear shape from brown construction paper or brown paper bags. The children brush glue across the bear shape and then shake dried tea leaves or coffee grounds across it. After shaking off the excess leaves, glue buttons or stickers on the bear for eyes and a nose.

Materials needed:
- dried tea leaves or dried coffee grounds
- buttons or stickers
- scissors
- glue

Bear Puppets

Use with older children (in grades 1 to 3). After you read the story, the children can create their own Corduroy puppets. Use brown paper lunch bags for the body of the puppet. Draw the upper part of the face on the upper part of the bag. The children can use their imaginations to add facial features, costumes, etc. The children can add arms, feet, ears, and hair to the puppets.

Materials needed:
- brown paper lunch bags

- colored paper
- glue
- scissors
- drawing materials

Related Books: Bears

Berenstain, Stan, and Jan Berenstain. **The Berenstain Bears** (series). New York: Random House. The Berenstains have created a multivolume series of books on the adventures of Mama and Papa Bear and their children, Sister and Brother.

Marshall, James. *Goldilocks and the Three Bears.* New York: Dial, 1988. This is a new version of an old tale.

Peet, Bill. *Big Bad Bruce.* Boston: Houghton Mifflin, 1977. Bruce, the bully bear, meets his match in Roxy, a spunky, foxy, little witch.

Waddell, Martin. *Can't You Sleep, Little Bear?* Illustrated by Barbara Firth. Cambridge, MA: Candlewick, 1992. Little Bear is afraid of the dark, and it takes a special solution from Father Bear to solve the problem.

Wildsmith, Brian. *The Lazy Bear.* New York: Watts, 1974. When the lazy bear tires of pushing the wagon up the hill after each ride, he schemes to have his friends do it for him.

Giveaways: Bear cookies and/or graham crackers, and fact sheet on bears

 Preparation time
Story: 5–10 min.
Optional Activities
    Fuzzy Wuzzy Bear: 15–25 min.
    Bear Puppets: 15–20 min.

Fuzzy Wuzzy Bears Pattern

The "Bare" Facts About Bears

Bears have:

- short strong legs
- large feet
- excellent sense of smell
- small eyes & poor eyesight
- life span of 15 to 30 years

Home is:

Arctic, Asia, North America, Europe, or South America

FACTS

The Alaskan brown bear is the biggest (9 feet—1500 pounds).
Bears spend most of the winter sleeping.
Grizzlies are the most dangerous bears (8 feet—800 pounds) and are called grizzlies because of the white hairs mixed in with their brown hair.
Bears have few enemies except other bears and humans.
American black bears are the most common.
Bears can have from one to four cubs, but usually have two at a time.
Polar bears are the best swimmers.

Types of Bears

Big Brown
American Black
Asiatic Black
Polar
Sun
Sloth
Spectacled

Favorite foods are:

ants, grubs, birds' eggs,
acorns, berries, fruit, nuts, leaves,
and roots of plants,
AND

they have a fondness for

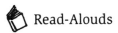

The Day Jimmy's Boa Ate the Wash

By Trinka Hakes Noble • Illustrated by Steven Kellogg

Dial, 1980

Summary: When the class goes on a field trip to a farm, Jimmy's pet boa constrictor turns the trip into a series of hilarious mishaps.

Procedure: The pictures in this hilarious tall tale are too irresistible not to share with the children. There are several ways to introduce the story to the audience. With young children (preschool to grade 1), introduce the story by asking the children if they know what a boa constrictor is. Explain that it is a very large snake and that in this story the boa constrictor causes some problems on a class trip. For older children, introduce the story by asking if they know what a tall tale is. Briefly discuss tall tales and how ordinary events are often greatly exaggerated in such stories. Another way to introduce the story is to talk about field trips. Ask the children to describe a field trip that they might have been involved with. Read the story aloud to the group, and let them enjoy the pictures.

To conclude the story time, have the children tell what they think happened after the bus left and Jimmy's boa constrictor was left on the farm.

Optional Activities

Make Your Own Boa Constrictor

Creating your own boa constrictor is a good activity for any age, and the activity can be as simple as making a string of different types of items or as complex as creating a fabric boa constrictor. For young children, make a boa constrictor by stringing pieces of straws, different types of beads, and various sizes of paper together to create a multidimensional boa constrictor. Each child can determine the length of his or her boa. You may wish to use modeling clay, felt, or fabric with older children to create a boa constrictor model. Shape the modeling clay into a snake or boa shape and decorate it. Fabric boa con-

strictors are created by cutting a piece of fabric to the size and length desired; sewing together three sides of the boa; stuffing the fabric with fiberfill, pieces of old panty hose, rags, or other materials; and sewing together the open end. Glue or sew on eyes, a nose and a mouth.

Materials needed for paper boa constrictors:
- string
- straws (cut in small pieces)
- colored paper (cut in various sizes & shapes)
- beads (include a multitude of sizes & shapes)
- scissors

Materials needed for clay boa constrictors:
- modeling clay
- paint
- old newspapers

Materials needed for fabric boa constrictors:
- fabric (any type)
- thread
- stuffing for boa (fiberfill, rags, etc.)
- felt

 Preparation time
Story: 5–10 min.
Optional Activities
Make Your Own Boa Constrictor:
    10–25 min. (depending on age of children.
What Happened Down on the Farm?
5–15 min.

What Happened Down on the Farm?
(activity sheet)

This is a drawing activity sheet on which each child completes the boa constrictor and tells what adventures it had down on the farm.

Related Books: Field Trips

Butterworth, Nick, and Mick Inkpen. *The School Trip.* New York: Delacorte, 1990. Miss Jefferson's class goes on a trip to the Natural History Museum, where they see bears, whales, lions, and have a great time.

Fleischman, Paul. *Time Train.* Illustrations by Claire Ewart. New York: HarperCollins, 1991. A class takes a trip through time to observe dinosaurs in their natural habitat.

Slater, Teddy. *Stay in Line.* Illustrated by Gioia Fiammenghi. New York: Cartwheel, 1996. Twelve children on a trip to the zoo group themselves into lines of different sizes.

Tyron, Leslie. *Albert's Field Trip.* New York: Atheneum, 1993. Albert takes the class on a field trip to an apple farm, where they pick apples, see apple juice being made, and eat apple pies.

Giveaway

Rope licorice (to remind the children of the boa constrictor)

What Happened Down on the Farm?

Jimmy's boa constrictor had many adventures on the
field trip to the farm.

Can you complete his body and tell about his adventures?

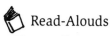

Ernest and Celestine's Picnic

by Gabrielle Vincent

Morrow, 1982

Summary: Despite the rain outside, Ernest and Celestine decide to go on their planned picnic.

Procedure: Ernest and Celestine are always favorites of the younger set, and this short picture book is perfect for a day when you have a limited amount of time for a story. Introduce the book by telling the children about Ernest, the bear, and Celestine, the mouse. They are two very good friends who are always going on adventures together. After you read the story, conclude by asking the children to relate some of their experiences on picnics.

Optional Activities

Let's Go on a Picnic (activity sheet)

Use this activity sheet either as a take home activity or as a group activity to follow the story. Have the children draw a large picnic basket sitting on a table-cloth in the center of the activity sheet (or in the case of a group activity, on a large piece of poster board). The children can draw and label some of the foods that they might take on a picnic. As an option you may give the children an activity sheet with the bas-ket drawn on it. This works best with preschoolers.

Materials needed:
- poster board or activity sheet
- pencils, crayons, and markers

Oh, Boy! A Picnic

As a special treat, have a picnic in the library after you read the story. Spread out a tablecloth on the floor, and bring out a picnic basket filled with picnic foods for the children. Give the children sandwich-es, cookies, fruit, etc., and tell them that just as Ernest and Celestine held a picnic with the rain out-side, we are having one in the library. As the group eats, discuss some of the things that happen on pic-nics, such as ants and other bugs invading, rain, food dropping, and things spilling.

Materials needed:
- tablecloth
- picnic basket
- enough food for the group (Keep it simple, for example, sandwiches, cookies, fruit, juice, veggie strips, etc.)

Related Books: Picnics

Kennedy, Jimmy. *The Teddy Bears' Picnic.* La Joffa, Calif.: Green Tiger, 1983. The lyrics of a familiar song provide the text for this story about the teddy bears going on a picnic in the woods.

McCully, Emily Arnold. *Picnic.* New York: Harper and Row, 1984. This is a wordless story about a family of mice on a picnic.

Miranda, Anne. *Pignic: An Alphabet Book in Rhyme.* Illustrated by Rosekrans Hoffman. Honesdale, PA: Boyds Mills, 1996. All the pigs bring their favorite dish to the annual "pignic" in this unique alphabet book.

Morton, Christine. *Picnic Farm.* Illustrated by Sarah Barringer. New York: Holiday House, 1998. When the children visit the farm, they learn all about the ingredients that make up their delicious picnic meal.

Welber, Robert. *The Winter Picnic.* New York: Pantheon, 1970. Adam's mother does not have time for a picnic until she sees all the elaborate prepara-tions that he has made.

Yeoman, John. *The Bear's Water Picnic.* Illustrated by Quentin Blake. New York: Atheneum, 1983. When a bear invites his friends—pig, squirrel, hedgehog, and hen—to go on a picnic on his raft, he does not expect to have any problems.

 Preparation time
Story: 5–10 min.
Optional Activities
 Let's Go on a Picnic: 10–20 min.
 Oh Boy! A Picnic: 10–25 min.

Let's Go on a Picnic

What things would you take on a picnic? Draw pictures of these items around the picnic basket.

Funnybones

by Janet and Allen Ahlberg
Greenwillow, 1980

Summary: This is a rhythmic tale of two skeletons and their dog going for a walk through the town one dark night.

Procedure: Introduce the story by asking the children if they like to take walks. Where do they go? What do they do? Then, make the transition to the story by saying you have a story about two skeletons who go for a walk and find all kinds of adventures along the way.

Optional Activities

Bone Bookmarks

Have each child draw an outline of a bone on white construction paper and cut it out. The children can use the bones as bookmarks. They can write the names of the bones on the bookmarks, for example, funny bone, elbow, chin bone, etc.

Materials needed:
- scissors
- white construction paper
- pencils

Walking Skeletons

Have the children draw skeleton bodies on poster board along with separate skeleton heads, arms, and legs. Cut out the skeleton parts. Attach the skeleton head, arms, and legs to the body using brass fasteners. These fasteners allow the head and limbs to move back and forth. Using a hole puncher, make a hole in the center of the head. Attach a string through the hole and you have a walking skeleton. The finished figures can range in size from 4 to 20 inches, depending on the skill of the children. If desired, give the children a copy of the activity sheet containing an outline of a skeleton.

Materials needed:
- white poster board
- markers, crayons, or pencils
- scissors
- string
- paper fasteners
- hole puncher

Related Books: Bones, Bones and More Bones

Barner, Bob. *Dem Bones.* New York: Scholastic, 1996. This picturebook rendition of an old rhyme gives information about the different bones.

Johnston, Tony. *The Soup Bone.* Illustrated by Margot Tomes. San Diego: Harcourt Brace Jovanovich, 1990. When a little old lady goes looking for a soup bone, she finds a skeleton and a friend instead.

Loredo, Elizabeth. *Boogie Bones.* Illustrated by Kevin Hawkes. New York: Putnam, 1997. Boogies Bones is a skeleton who loves to dance, so he disguises himself as a person to enter a dance contest.

Nikola-Lisa, W. *Shake Dem Halloween Bones.* Boston: Houghton Mifflin, 1997. All sorts of fairy tale characters attend a rapping, stomping, shaking, hip-hop Halloween ball.

 Preparation time
Story: 5–10 min.
Optional Activities
  Bone Bookmarks: 5–15 min.
  Walking Skeletons: 10–20 min.

Bone Bookmark Pattern

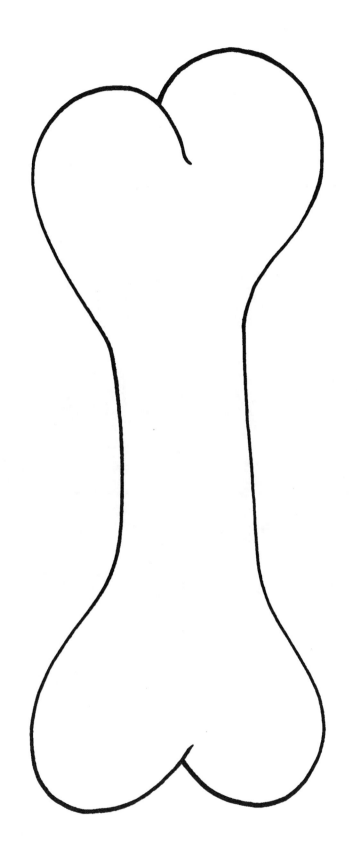

Walking Skeletons

Glue skeleton sheet to cardboard and cut out parts. Punch holes at the numbers, and join together with paper fasteners. Attach a string at the top of the skull to make a walking skeleton.

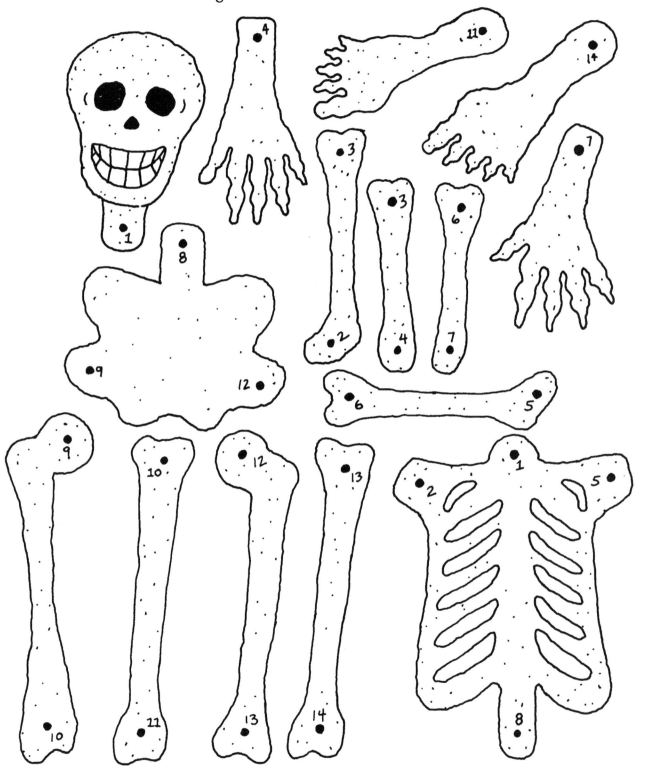

Read-Alouds

The Giant Carrot

by Jan Peck
Dial, 1998

Summary: Little Isabelle uses a special method to help a carrot seed grow into a huge vegetable.

Procedure: Before reading the story, ask the children if anyone has ever planted seeds and watched them grow into vegetables or plants. Lead into the story by saying that Little Isabelle uses some very special techniques to make a tiny little carrot seed turn into carrot pudding.

Optional Activities

The Giant _____

Write a story about a giant vegetable or fruit. Give each child the story starter sheet and have them write and illustrate their own story about a giant plant.

What Can You Do With a Carrot?

After reading the story, brainstorm ideas on ways to use the giant carrot. Find recipes that call for carrots as the main ingredient. Have the students try some of the recipes including carrot cake and the carrot pudding recipe on the last page of the picture book. Copy the recipes on carrot-shaped paper and make a carrot cookbook. Include other ideas for using carrots other than as a food ingredient.

Materials needed:
- cookbooks
- card stock paper cut in carrot shapes
- pencil, pen or other writing tools

Related Books: Bigger than Life

Mimmelman, John. *Amanda and Her Magic Garden.* New York: Viking Kestrel, 1987. Amanda uses magic seeds in her garden, but she doesn't know what to do when the animals who eat the vegetable s grow to giant size.

Milhouse, Katherine, and Alice Dalgiesh. *The Turnip: An Old Russian Folktale.* New York: Putnam, 1990. This picture book relates the old tale of a procession of colorful characters who try to pull a turnip out of the ground.

Morgan, Pierr. *The Turnip.* New York: Philomel, 1990. When one of Dedoushka's turnips grows to an enormous size, the whole family tries to pull it out of the ground.

Silverman, Erica. *Big Pumpkin.* Illustrated by S.D. Schindler. New York: Macmillan, 1992. When a witch tries to pick a big pumpkin, she has to ask for help from a series of monsters.

Westcott, Nadien Bernard. *The Giant Vegetable Garden.* Boston: Little, Brown, 1981. The townspeople are so determined to win the fair prize for the finest vegetables, that they let their gardens grow until the giant vegetables threaten to strangle the village.

Giveaway

Servings of carrot pudding

Preparation time
Story: 5–15 min.
Optional Activities
  The Giant _____: 10–25 min.
  What Can You Do With a Carrot?
    10–30 min.

The Giant _____

Isabelle's singing and dancing helped make the carrot grow in *The Giant Carrot*. Choose a vegetable or flower and write a story about what happens when it grows to a gigantic size.

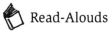

The Giant Jam Sandwich

Story and illustrations by John Vernon Lord
Verses by Janet Burroway
Houghton Mifflin, 1972

Summary: A small village afflicted by a plague of wasps solves the problem by creating a giant jam sandwich.

Procedure: As you recite the rollicking verses in this rhythmic tale, show the pictures to your audience.

Optional Activity

Balloon Wasps

The children create their own nest of wasps by turning yellow balloons into a hive of them. Give each child a yellow balloon. You may want to have them already blown up and tied with a string.

To create wasps, draw stripes around the balloons using markers. (Or, if you are really brave and do not mind the mess, let the children paint stripes on the balloons.) Draw on eyes with black markers or stick on black color coding dots for eyes.

Additional features that the children might like to add include pipe cleaner stingers and antennas and paper wings. Attach strings to the tied end of the balloon. When finished, the children can toss the balloon insects in the air and let them buzz around the room.

Materials needed:

- yellow balloons
- black markers
- string
- black circle stickers (color coding labels work well)
- black construction paper (for wings)
- pipe cleaners
- scissors

Related Books: Jams and Jellies

Degen, Bruce. *Jamberry.* New York: Harper and Row, 1983. A rhyming tale of a boy and a bear who go on a berry-picking adventure.

Hoban, Russell. ***Bread and Jam for Frances.*** Illustrated by Lilian Hoban. New York: Harper, 1964. When Frances refuses to eat anything but bread and jam, her mother lets her eat it with some surprising results.

Josse, Barbara M. *Jam Day.* Illustrated by Emily Arnold McCully. New York: Harper, 1987. At the family reunion, everyone helps pick berries and make jam.

Mahy, Margaret. *Jam: A True Story.* Illustrated by Helen Craig. Boston: Atlantic Monthly Press, 1985. One day when the plums are ripe, Mr. Castle decides to make some jam.

Taylor, Judy. ***Dudley In a Jam.*** Illustrated by Peter Cross. New York: Putnam, 1986. Dudley Dormouse tries to make plum jam and discovers that it can be a sticky business.

Westcott, Nadine Bernard. ***Peanut Butter and Jelly.*** New York: Dutton, 1987. This is a picturebook version of an old finger play.

Giveaway

What else—*Jam sandwiches!*

Preparation time
Story: 5–10 min.
Optional Activities
Balloon Wasps: 10–20 min.

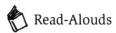
If You Give a Mouse a Cookie

By Laura Joffe Numeroff • Illustrated by Felicia Bond

Harper, 1985

Summary: When a little boy gives a mouse a cookie, he sets off a chain of astonishing events in this truly delightful picture book.

Procedure: The pictures in this book are so captivating that it would be a shame not to share them with your audience. The text is brief, so read very slowly and make sure all the children can see the pictures. This story has a built-in rhyme that is very easy to pick up after reading once or twice.

Introduce the story by asking the children if they have a favorite kind of cookie. Listen to some of the answers and comment on them. Lead into the story by saying one of your favorite kinds of cookies is chocolate chip like the mouse in the story *If You Give a Mouse a Cookie.*

Optional Activities

Milk and Cookie Feast

As a tie-in to the story, treat the children to a milk and chocolate chip cookies feast while they discuss what they might have done in the little boy's place.

> *Materials needed:*
> - chocolate chip cookies
> - small glasses of milk

Cookie Decorating

If you have a small group of children, let the children decorate cookies with faces.

> *Materials needed:*
> - cookies (sugar cookies work best)
> - decorating materials (including icing, sprinkles, colored sugar, and assorted small candies)

Where's the Cookie? (activity sheet)

Give each child a cookie maze activity sheet to take home.

Related Books: Cookies

Douglass, Barbara. *The Chocolate Chip Cookie Contest.* New York: Lothrop, Lee & Shepard, 1985. Cory and Kevin learn to make prize-winning chocolate chip cookies with a little help from family and friends.

Hutchins, Pat. *The Doorbell Rang.* New York: Greenwillow, 1986. The children have to divide and share their cookies with friends stopping by, when they run out of cookies, Grandma comes to the rescue.

Lindgren, Barbro. *Sam's Cookie.* New York: Morrow, 1982. Sam loses his cookie to his dog.

Rix, Jamie. *The Last Chocolate Cookie.* Illustrated by Arthur Robins. Cambridge, MA: Candlewick, 1997. When Maurice takes the last cookie, his mother tells him to offer it to everyone with some amazing results.

Wellington, Monica. *Mr. Cookie Baker.* New York: Dutton, 1992. After a long day of making cookies, Mr Cookie Baker finally gets to eat a cookie.

Giveaways

Chocolate chip cookies, of course, and "Where's the Cookie?" activity sheet

Preparation time
Story: 5–10 min.
Optional Activities
Milk & Cookie Feast: 5–10 min.
Mosaic Turtles: 10–20 min.
(unless cookies are baked from scratch)
Cookie Decorating: 15–20 min.
Where's the Cookie? 5–10 min.

Where's the Cookie?

What happens if you give a mouse a cookie? Follow the mouse along the path to find out what happens. Do not cross any lines along the way.

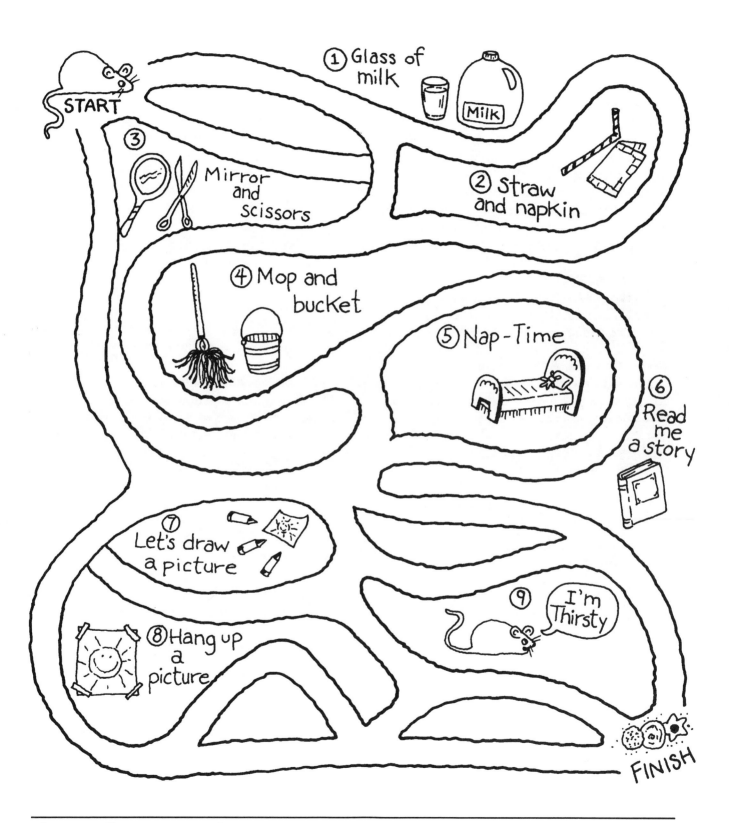

The Magic Bubble Trip

by Ingrid and Dieter Schubert
Kane/Miller, 1985

Summary: When James blows a giant bubble, he finds himself carried away to the land of giant hairy frogs.

Procedure: Introduce this story by talking about soap bubbles, how to blow them, how much fun they are to make, etc. Ask the children if they have ever blown soap bubbles. Keep the anecdotes as brief as possible. Lead into the story by saying, "In this story, James blows a giant bubble that carries him away." Then, read the story to the children.

Optional Activities

Matchbox Frogs

Have the children make frogs from matchboxes to resemble the box frog in the story. Give each child a matchbox and green pipe cleaners. Turn the matchbox on its side and either cover it with green paper or paint it green. While the box is drying, have the children cut the pipe cleaners into four equal parts to use as legs for the frog. Cut green yarn into small pieces to use as hair. (With younger children, you need to have the yarn already cut into small pieces.) Slightly bend one end of the pipe cleaners and insert them into the bottom of the box as the frog's legs. Glue buttons on the front of the box for eyes, and draw or paint other facial features. Glue the yarn on the frog for hair.

Materials needed:
- matchboxes
- green and black paint
- paintbrushes
- green yarn
- green pipe cleaners
- green construction paper and other scraps
- scissors
- glue
- markers and crayons

Giant Hairy Frogs

This activity is best used with preschoolers through first graders. Cut frog shapes from green construction paper. Cut four strips for legs and accordion fold the strips. Attach legs to the bottom of the frog's body. Cut green yarn into small pieces, and glue the pieces to the frog to make hair. Draw facial features on the frog. Attach a piece of elastic string to the main body of the frog to complete the giant hairy jumping frog.

Materials needed:
- green construction paper
- tape and/or glue
- scissors
- green yarn
- elastic string
- crayons and/or markers

Let's Make Soap Bubbles

Mix dishwashing liquid, water, and glycerin together. Wet the surface of a counter or table with the soap solution. Dip a straw into the soap, and leaning over the surface, blow gently through the straw. After one or two tries, a bubble will begin to grow. Let the children experiment with blowing bubbles as large as they can, bubbles within bubbles, etc.

Preparation time
Story: 5–10 min.
Optional Activities
  Matchbox Frogs: 15–30 min.
  Giant Hairy Frogs: 5–15 min.
  Let's Make Soap Bubbles: 5–15 min.
  Blow a Magic Bubble: 5–15 min.

Materials needed:
- plastic drinking straws
- ½ cup of high-quality dishwashing liquid
- 8 cups of water
- glycerin (optional)

Blow a Magic Bubble

This is an alternate activity if you do not have time for "Let's Make Soap Bubbles." Give each child a small cup filled with soap bubble mix and a bubble blower. Show the children how to blow bubbles. Then, hold a contest to see who can blow the biggest bubble.

Materials needed:
- soap bubble mix
- bubble blowers

Related Books: Bubbles

dePaola, Tomie. ***The Bubble Factory.*** New York: Grosset & Dunlap, 1996. Grampa takes Sam and Molly to the Bubble Factory where they accidently create wish bubbles.

Everett, Louise. ***Bubble Gum in the Sky.*** Illustrated by Paul Harvey. Mahwah, NJ: Troll Associates, 1988. A rabbit blows a gigantic bubble gum bubble only to have it carry him away into the sky.

Mater, Mercer. ***Bubble Bubble.*** New York: Rainbird, 1973. A little boy buys a magic bubble maker that creates all sorts of unusual creatures.

Nolan, Dennis. ***Monster Bubbles.*** Englewood Cliffs, NJ: Prentice-Hall, 1976. A series of monsters blow bubbles in this counting book that covers one to twenty.

Giveaways

Bubble blowers and bubble mix

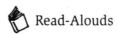 Read-Alouds

Meanwhile Back at the Ranch

By Trinka Hakes Noble • Illustrated by Tony Ross
Dial, 1987

Summary: When Rancher Hicks goes to town seeking excitement while his wife stays home to dig potatoes, he returns to find that the real excitement was on his ranch.

Procedure: Introduce the story by asking the children if they know what a tall tale is. Discuss the term and how tall tales are very much a part of America's heritage. Lead into the story by explaining to the children that this story is a tall tale. The pictures and humor in this story are irresistible and are guaranteed hits with the seven- to nine-year-old crowd.

Optional Activities

Tall Tale Word Find (activity sheet)
After telling the children about some of the famous American tall tale heroes, give them this word puzzle featuring some of them.

Wacky Tall Tales
This activity is best used with second graders and up. Tell the children that you would like for each of them to write a tall tale and to bring it with them on their next visit. Give them a line to start with, and let each child's imagination take it from there. You might start with "Meanwhile back at the _____."

Related Books: The Far-Fetched

Barrett, Judi. *Cloudy with a Chance of Meatballs.* Illustrated by Ron Barrett. New York: Atheneum, 1984. In the town of Chew and Swallow, food falls from the sky.

Kellogg, Steven. *Pecos Bill.* New York: Dial, 1976. This is a read-aloud version of the legend of Pecos Bill.

Purdy, Carol. *Iva Dunnitt and the Big Wind.* Illustrated by Steven Kellogg. New York: Dial, 1985. A pioneer woman and her six children struggle to save their home during a ferocious windstorm.

Root, Phyllis. *Rosie's Fiddle.* Illustrated by Kevin O'Malley. New York: Lothrop, Lee & Shepard, 1997. Rosie O'Grady can out fiddle the devil himself, and one day the devil challenges her to a contest.

Williams, Suzanne. *Library Lil.* Illustrated by Steven Kellogg. New York: Dial, 1997. When Lil turns a resistant town into avid readers, she also has a formidable foe in a tough-talking television-watching motorcycle gang and their leader Bust-'em-up Bill.

 Preparation time
Story—5–10 min.
Optional Activities
    Tall Tale Word Find 10–15 min.
    Wacky Tall Tales varies

Tall Tale Word Find

Unlike fairy tales that are about strange lands and kings and queens, tall tales and legends are stories about ordinary people with ordinary jobs. However, a tall tale or legend exaggerates everyday people and events into the extraordinary.

Following is a list of some famous American folk heroes and legends. See if you can find all 12 characters in the word search. You may find the answers across, up, down, or diagonally.

```
J  O  H  N  N  Y  A  P  P  L  E  S  E  E  D
P  A  U  L  B  U  N  Y  A  N  O  P  R  E  A
E  S  M  L  Y  W  N  Y  Q  K  L  M  N  N  V
C  E  I  M  R  O  I  R  X  S  A  L  J  O  Y
O  M  K  W  T  U  E  N  Z  V  B  O  Y  O  C
S  A  E  T  B  N  O  E  P  W  I  N  M  B  R
B  J  F  P  O  C  A  H  O  N  T  A  S  L  O
I  E  I  T  Y  J  K  N  C  V  F  E  W  E  C
L  S  N  R  E  W  L  H  M  R  Y  P  M  I  K
L  S  K  T  R  U  E  O  M  C  V  H  U  N  E
W  E  C  A  S  E  Y  J  O  N  E  S  L  A  T
Y  J  S  B  I  L  L  Y  T  H  E  K  I  D  T
```

Johnny Appleseed

Pecos Bill

Billy the Kid

Daniel Boone

Paul Bunyan

Davy Crockett

Mike Fink

John Henry

Jesse James

Casey Jones

Annie Oakley

Pocahontas

No Peas for Nellie

by Chris L. Demarest
Macmillan, 1988

Summary: When Nellie is served peas, she imagines all sorts of things that she would rather eat than the peas on her plate.

Procedure: Because this story is short, read it slowly and use the voice to accentuate the things that Nellie would rather eat than her peas. Follow the story with a question and answer session about foods that the children would rather not eat.

Optional Activities

Pea Pods

Give each child a sheet of lightweight cardboard to use as a base for the project.

Cut out a pea pod shape from green felt and several pea-shaped figures. Cut a slit in the center of the pea pod. Place glue along the edges of the pod and glue it in the center of the cardboard. Glue a strip of Velcro to the cardboard inside the slit. Attach the other part of the Velcro strip to the peas using glue. The children can then add or remove the peas from the pod. Add details to the rest of the sheet to make it resemble a vegetable garden.

Materials needed:
- lightweight cardboard
- green felt
- scissors
- glue and/or paste
- Velcro strips
- coloring medium

None for Me, Thanks! (activity sheet)
Give each child an activity sheet to complete.

Related Materials: Picky Eaters

Hoban, Russell. *Bread and Jam for Frances.* Illustrated by Lilian Hoban. New York: Harper, 1964. When Frances refuses to eat anything but bread and jam, her mother lets her eat it with some interesting results.

Paterson, Diane. *Eat!* New York: Dial, 1975. When a little girl refuses to eat ordinary foods, her parents let her eat whatever she wants.

Rayner, Mary. *Mrs. Pig's Bulk Buy.* New York: Atheneum, 1981. When Mrs. Pig's children refuse to eat anything without catsup, she devises a way to change their minds.

Sharmat, Mitchell. *Gregory the Terrible Eater.* New York: Four Winds, 1980. When Gregory refuses to eat any junk foods, his parents take him to a doctor.

Preparation time
Story: 5–10 min.
Optional Activities
Pea Pods: 10–20 min.
None for Me, Thanks! 5–10 min.

None for Me, Thanks!

Draw a picture of the vegetable that Nellie didn't like to eat. What foods would you rather not eat? Draw pictures of some of them.

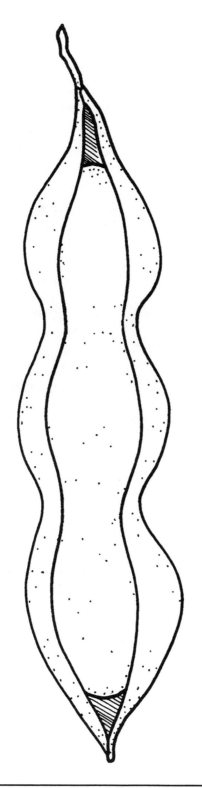

Oh, Were They Ever Happy!

by Peter Spier
Doubleday, 1978

Summary: When their parents go away for the day and the babysitter fails to come, three children decide to paint their house as a surprise for their parents.

Procedure: Peter Spier's watercolor illustrations are so detailed and interesting that is it best to use this book as a read-aloud. As you read the story, be sure that each child can see the illustrations. Either after or just before you read the final page, ask the children what would happen if they painted their houses while their parents were away.

Optional Activities

Depending upon the age of the group and the amount of time you have left after the story, there are several activities that you can use in connection with this story.

Let's Paint a House

If you have a small group and lots of extra time, have a very large piece of white paper ready for the children to paint or draw on. You can have the outline of a large house on the paper and tell the children that they can paint the house any way they would like.

> *Materials needed:*
> - large piece of white paper containing an outline of a house
> - paint, crayons, or markers
> - paintbrushes
> - newspapers
> - old rags

Paint a House

If time is short or you have a large group, give each child an activity sheet with the outline of a house drawn on it, or have the children draw their own versions of the house. Tell the children that like the children in the story, they may paint the house in any way that they would like. You may choose to hang the children's drawings on a bulletin board with the title "Oh, Were They Ever Happy!"

Related Books: Let's Paint!

Baker, Alan. *Black and White Rabbit's ABC*. New York: Kingfisher, 1994. A rabbit wears himself out trying to paint a picture that presents the letters of the alphabet.

Kellogg, Steven. *The Mystery of the Stolen Blue Paint*. New York: Dial, 1982. When the last bit of blue paint disappears, a little girl tries to track down the culprit.

Pinkwater, Daniel. *The Big Orange Splot*. New York: Hastings, 1972. When a big orange paint spot is dropped on Mr. Plumbean's house, he decides to use this opportunity to create his dream house.

Testa, Fulvio. *If You Take a Paintbrush*. New York: Dial, 1982. This book contains some ideas for creating things with a paintbrush.

Walsh, Ellen Stoll. *Mouse Paint*. San Diego: Harcourt Brace, 1994. When the mice find jars of paint, they have a ball experimenting with colors and designs until a cat interrupts their fun.

Preparation time
Story: 5–10 min.
Optional Activities
    Let's Paint a House: 15–25 min.
    Paint a House: 10–20 min.

On Market Street

By Arnold Lobel • Illustrated by Anita Lobel
Greenwillow, 1981

Summary: When a little girl goes to Market Street, she finds herself on a wondrous shopping spree of things from A to Z.

Procedure: Introduce the story by asking the children whether they like to go shopping. Lead into the story by saying that in this story a little girl is looking for a present on Market Street for a friend. At the beginning of the story, read in a normal voice, but slow down considerably as you go through the items that the girl finds in the shops. As you read the story, have the children try to guess what the girl bought that begins with the next letter of the alphabet. For example, for the letters A and B, tell the children what the girl bought. Then, ask the group to try to decide what she saw that begins with the letters C and D. By your alternating the telling and asking, the children are able to maintain an interest in the story and have fun thinking of things that begin with the letters of the alphabet.

Optional Activities

An A to Z Book Project

Explain that the children are going to create pages for an ABC book of things to buy at the stores in your town. Each child selects a letter of the alphabet for his or her page and puts pictures on the page of things that begin with the selected letter. The pictures can be drawn freehand or cut from magazines and newspapers. When finished, each child's page is put on display before the group. You can take all the completed pages and place them into book format to display during the next story time.

Materials needed:
- white drawing paper
- scissors
- glue and/or paste
- pencils, pens, markers, and crayons
- old magazines and/or newspapers

ABC Shopping Carts (activity sheet)

Give each child an activity sheet containing the outline of a shopping cart. The children then cut out the cart and place a letter of the alphabet on the back of the cart. They can draw or cut out pictures of things to buy that begin with that letter and place them in the shopping cart.

Materials needed:
- activity sheet with picture of shopping cart
- scissors
- coloring medium
- old magazines
- glue and/or paste

Grocery Shopping

Because this activity is more complex than the others and requires a great deal of time, it is a good one to suggest that a teacher or parent do. You can set up an ABC grocery store center in the classroom or in the library. Have the children create cards that have pictures of items found in the grocery store. Each card will have a letter of the alphabet on one side and a picture of an item beginning with that letter on the other. The pictures can be cut from newspapers and magazines or drawn on the cards. You can also include play foods and fruits and vegetables, as well as empty cans with labels on them. Children practice putting things in alphabetical order using the cards and play foods.

Preparation time
Story: 5–10 min.
Optional Activities
An A to Z Book Project: 10–20 min.
ABC Shopping Carts: 5–20 min.
Grocery Shopping: 30–60 min.

Materials needed:
- index cards of assorted colors (4"x6")
- old magazines and/or newspapers
- scissors
- glue and/or paste
- plastic fruits and vegetables
- old cans with labels
- play foods
- coloring medium

Related Books: Oh Boy! Shopping Time

Aylesworth, Jim. *McGraw's Emporium.* Pictures by Mavis Smith. New York: Holt, 1995. A little boy searches for a gift in McGraw's Emporium, but finally settles on a free kitten as his special present.

Edwards, Linda Strauss. *The Downtown Day.* New York: Pantheon, 1983. Linda's aunts take her downtown to shop for new school clothes.

Gretz, Susanna. *Teddy Bears Go Shopping.* New York: Four Winds, 1982. The teddy bears make a list of things to get at the store only to lose the list and forget some things.

Patz, Nancy. *Pumpernickel Tickle and Mean Green Cheese.* New York: Watts, 1978. Benjamin and Elephant create fantastic food rhymes and puns on their way to the store to help them remember their grocery list.

Shaw, Nancy. *Sheep In a Store.* Illustrated by Margot Apple. Boston: Houghton Mifflin, 1991. When the sheep go shopping, they have to take drastic measures to pay for their purchases.

ABC Shopping Cart

Cut out the square containing the shopping cart and glue it to a piece of card-board. On the back of the cart write a letter of the alphabet. Draw or cut out pictures of things that you could buy that begin with that letter. Place them in the shopping cart.

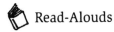

Read-Alouds
Pizza for Breakfast

By Mary Ann Kovalski • Illustrated by Anita Lobel
Morrow Junior, 1990

Summary: Frank and Zelda discover that wishing for more customers (all day and night) only create more problems.

Procedures: Share a little bit of background history on pizza with the children before reading the story aloud. To introduce the story, talk about wishes and how sometimes they are not always what we think they are. Lead into the story by saying that Frank and Zelda's wishes come true, but not in the way that they wanted.

Optional Activities

Pizza Bookmarks

Give each child a copy of the pizza slice pattern. Have the children draw their favorite toppings on the slice and even cut out and glue pictures of toppings from magazines. Color the handdrawn illustrations, cut out the pizza slice, and laminate the bookmarks for more permanent use.

Materials needed:
- pizza slice pattern
- coloring medium
- scissors
- old magazines (optional)
- glue

My Pizza Story

Make pizza-shape books using the pizza slice pattern for the cover and pages. Let each child write a story about an adventure that he or she has had with pizza, a list of favorite toppings, or even another ending to the *Pizza for Breakfast* story. Be sure to include some illustrations throughout the story. Cut out the pizza slice pages and staple together.

Materials needed:
- pizza slice pattern
- coloring medium
- scissors
- stapler and staples

Mini Pizzas

Let each child make a mini pizza using English muffins and a wide assortment of possible toppings such as pepperoni, cheeses, olives, tomato sauce, sausage, and others. Bake the mini pizzas in a toaster oven or regular oven, and share them for snacks.

Materials needed:
- English muffins
- assorted toppings
- oven

Related Books: We Love Pizza!

Barbour, Karen. *Little Nino's Pizzeria.* San Diego: Harcourt Brace Jovanovich, 1987. Despite the success of his father's fancy new business, Tony misses the fun he had at the old pizzeria.

Khlasha, Dayal Kaur. *How Pizza Came to Queens.* New York: Clarkson N. Potter, 1989. When Mrs. Pelligrino arrives from Italy, she is disappointed to find no pizza, a situation she quickly decides to change.

Krensky, Stephen. *The Pizza Man.* Illustrated by R. W. Alley. New York: Scholastic, 1992. As a father and daughter make pizza, they learn all sorts of facts and fancy about this popular food.

Maccarone, Grace. *Pizza Party!* Illustrated by Emily Arnold McCully. New York: Scholastic, 1994. A group of children have tons of fun making pizzas at their party.

 Preparation time
Story: 10–20 min.
Optional Activities
   Pizza Bookmarks: 5–15 min.
   My Pizza Story: 5–20 min.
   Mini Pizzas: 5–30 min.

Pizza Slice Pattern

Use the pizza slice pattern to make bookmarks, book covers, and other pizza creations.

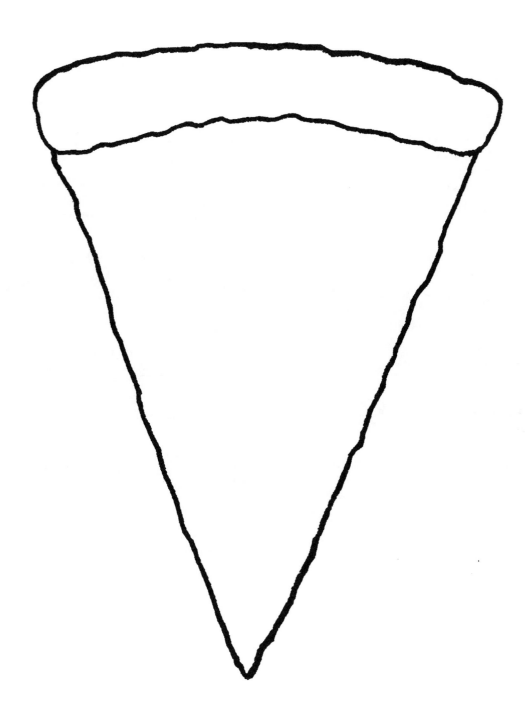

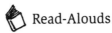 Read-Alouds

Three Days on a River in a Red Canoe

by Vera Williams

Morrow, 1986

Summary: Mother, her two children and Aunt Rose go on a three-day camping trip down the river.

Procedures: The story may be presented strictly as a read-aloud while showing the pictures to your audience. An alternative method would be to have a large posterboard map of the trip down the river. Mark significant spots on the map, and as you read the story, point out the groups progress by indicating spots on the map. (For example, point out the spot where the travelers have lunch on the top of the cliff.)

Optional Activities

Talk About Camping

After reading the story, ask the children if anyone has been on a camping trip. Let each child tell a little about his or her trip. Ask what kinds of things the children took on their trips and then compare their lists to the list of things the book characters took on their trip.

Mapping Out the Canoe Trip

Make a map showing the river trip. Include a list of high points that the author mentions in the story. Tell the children that they can mark the points on their copies of the map. Have a start and finish point. This activity is good to use in connection with the storytelling alternative that involves using a posterboard map.

Materials needed:

- copies of the river trip map, with a list of 14 trip high points
- pencils or crayons

Related Books: Camp Out

Brown, Marc. *Arthur Goes to Camp.* Boston: Little, Brown, 1982. Arthur, the aardvark, learns all about camp.

Parish, Peggy. *Amelia Bedelia Goes Camping.* New York: Avon Camelot, 1985. When Amelia Bedelia goes on a camping trip, all kinds of unusual things begin to happen.

Warren, Cathy. *The Ten-Alarm Camp-Out.* New York: Lothrop, Lee & Shepard, 1983. The armadillo family innocently creates chaos on its overnight camp-out.

Yolen, Jane. *The Giants Go Camping.* New York: Clarion Books, 1979. The escapades of five giants who decide to go on a camping trip to the mountains.

Giveaways

"Some-mores" and the recipe

"Some-mores"

Put a piece of chocolate (such as a part of a Hershey bar) on top of a graham cracker. Toast one or two marshmallows and place the marshmallows on top of the chocolate. Top with another graham cracker.

 Preparation time

Story: 5–10 min.

Optional Activities

Talk About Camping: 5–15 min.

Mapping Out the Canoe Trip: 5–15 min.

The Unbeatable Bread

by Lyn Littlefield Hoopes

Dial, 1996

Summary: Uncle Jon bakes a magical, spell-binding bread that brings people and animals to join in a fabulous feast.

Procedure: The wonderful rhythm and rich three-dimensional illustrations in this book make it a perfect read-aloud for a cold winter day. To really set the mood, arrange to have the scent of freshly baked bread in the air. Begin the story by asking the audience if anyone has ever baked bread. Tell the children the story is about an "unbeatable" bread that breaks the spell of a frozen snowy town. As you read the story to the children, encourage them to repeat the phrases that occur throughout the tale. Afterwards, discuss the smells and tastes associated with freshly baked breads and other goods, different types of breads, and things to put on and eat with bread.

Optional Activities

Breads for Sale

One activity to use with younger children is to create plates of bread. Instead of using real materials, give each child a paper plate. Each child cuts out pictures of different breads and glues them on his or her paper plate, creating a plate of breads for sale.

Materials needed:

- paper plates
- old magazines
- scissors
- glue or glue sticks

Bread, Bread, Bread and More

Divide the audience into groups of three to five each. Have the children brainstorm a list of breads that they have eaten. Make a chart of the list and categorize that list by types, forms or grain or cereal. Have each group share their findings.

Materials needed:

- paper
- pencil or other writing tools

Paper Breads

This activity is better suited for older children and involves more than one session to complete. Each child will make papier-mâché breads. Tear old newspapers into 1"-wide strips. Mix equal parts of flour and water together in a bowl and soak the strips in the mixture. Use the soaked newspaper strips to create different shapes of breads such as loaves, rolls, and slices. Let the shapes dry overnight and then paint them with white, brown, tan or yellow tempera paints.

Materials needed:

- old newspapers
- flour
- water
- tempera paints
- paint brushes

Preparation time

Story: 5–15 min.

Optional Activities

Bread for Sale: 15–30 min.

Bread, Bread, Bread and More: 15–30 min.

Paper Breads: 1–3 hours

Related Books: Wonderful Breads

dePaola, Tomie. ***Tony's Bread.*** New York: Putnam, 1989. Tony bakes panettone, a special kind of bread, which earns him a bakery in the grand city of Milano. But he loses his daughter to a determined nobleman.

Morris, Ann. ***Bread Bread Bread.*** Photographs by Ken Hayman. New York: Lothrop, Lee & Shepard, 1989. Photographs and simple text are used to show the many different kinds of breads found all around the world.

Myers, Edward. ***Forri the Baker.*** Pictures by Alexi Natchev. New York: Dial, 1995. When the Chlars invade this peaceful village, Forri, the baker, devises an ingenious plan to save the townspeople.

Wolff, Ferida. ***Seven Loaves of Bread.*** Picture by Katie Keller. New York: Tambourine Books, 1993. When Milly, who does all the baking, gets sick, Rose takes over and has to mend her lazy ways before the farm goes to seed.

Giveaway

"Find That Bread" activity sheet

Find That Bread

Find and circle all the different types of bread in the puzzle. You will find words up or down, across, backwards or diagonally.

```
P  U  M  P  E  R  N  I  C  K  E  L
O  S  J  A  F  U  A  T  I  P  L  P
C  O  R  N  B  R  E  A  D  O  M  E
K  D  Y  E  G  C  E  Y  R  U  B  T
E  A  T  T  O  R  T  I  L  L  A  S
T  B  I  T  M  O  L  Y  W  B  G  E
B  R  U  O  U  I  E  C  H  U  U  I
R  E  C  N  F  S  G  N  E  R  E  T
E  A  S  E  F  S  A  E  A  R  T  T
A  D  I  U  I  A  B  R  T  I  T  A
D  V  B  A  N  N  O  C  K  T  E  P
O  Z  T  A  M  T  I  N  J  O  R  P
M  I  L  L  E  T  C  A  K  E  S  A
W  H  I  T  E  C  H  A  L  L  A  H
M  F  L  A  T  B  R  E  A  D  S  C
```

bagel	chappatties	millet cakes	pumpernickel
baguette	cornbread	muffin	roll
bannock	cracker	naan	rye
biscuit	croissant	nut	soda bread
bun	flatbreads	panettone	tortilla
burrito	inferra	pita	wheat
challah	matzo	pocket bread	white

Tagboard Stories

Tagboard stories are based on the same principle as flash cards. Just as using flash cards reinforces mathematics and reading skills, telling tagboard stories reinforces the plot and characters. Tagboard is a type of lightweight cardboard used for posters, artwork, mountings, etc. Tagboard is commonly found in art and educational supply stores. Most schools purchase tagboard in large quantities for use in classroom art projects. It is relatively inexpensive, comes in several sizes, and is usually found in white and manila.

There are several advantages to using tagboard rather than heavier weight poster board or drawing paper, including the following:

- Tagboard is inexpensive.
- Tagboard is lightweight, which makes it easy to laminate using either cold or hot lamination procedures.
- The surface of tagboard is receptive to many art materials such as watercolors, markers, crayons, tempera paints, and other readily available supplies.
- Tagboard is lightweight, so it is easy to hold up or place on an easel while relating the story to the children.

If you do not have access to tagboard, lightweight drawing paper or heavier poster board will work.

Creating a tagboard story is very easy. The only requirements are a story, tagboard, and some art materials. When choosing a story, select one with very simple illustrations that can be drawn easily or transferred to the tagboards. If you prefer, use the opaque projector or overhead projector to enlarge the design and to draw directly on the tagboard. After you have transferred or drawn the illustrations for the story, write the text on the back of the board. Number your illustrations in the order in which you will use them. Tagboard stories can require one to forty sheets of illustrations. Preparing a tagboard story can take thirty minutes to two hours, depending on the number and complexity of the illustrations.

You may choose to use only a few of the illustrations from the story or all of them. Use your own judgment when adapting a story for tagboard use.

As you relate the story to the children, hold up the appropriate tagboard illustration and either read the text from the back of the tagboard or retell it from memory. You may want to place the tagboard on an easel.

Although tagboard stories are the primary focus of this section, there are two other storytelling methods that are closely related to them. Both chalk talks and fold-and-tell stories can be used as a method of story presentation.

Chalk Talks

A chalk talk, or draw-and-tell, is a story relating a sequence of events through pictures. It is a very popular method of storytelling and can be used with children of all ages. Chalk and a blackboard are used to illustrate the story. The story begins with a simple line drawn on the blackboard, and as the plot develops, so does the picture. Instead of using chalk and a blackboard, you can use drawing pencils, charcoal, or markers and a drawing pad or cardboard to illustrate the story.

A good chalk talk is challenging and provides suspense and surprises for listeners. Younger children are often surprised at the finished picture, while older children try to guess what the picture will be by using visual and contextual clues.

No special artistic talent is needed to become a proficient chalk talk storyteller. Begin with one simple line and add more as the plot develops. The drawings are easy to remember and to do because they are directly related to the story. However, the storyteller needs to memorize the sequence of events and to practice the drawing beforehand.

With some editing and practice, you can develop your own chalk, or draw-and-tell, stories. The only materials needed are (1) imagination, chalk, and a blackboard or (2) imagination, markers, and an easel. Several books that contain ready-made chalk talks follow: *Elementary School Library Resource Kit* by Jerry J. Mallett and Marian R. Bartch; *Terrific Tales to Tell* by Valerie Marsh; *Tell and Draw Stories* and *More Tell and Draw Stories* by Margaret Oldfield; *The Story Vine* by Anne Pellowski; and *Chalk in Hand: The Draw and Tell Book* by Phyllis Pflomm.

Fold-and-Cut Stories

As a storyteller, you may want to use fold-and-cut stories, which involve folding and cutting paper as the story progresses. When the story ends, reveal the final product, which is directly linked to the story. Fold-and-cut stories are easy to remember because the cuts follow the sequence of events in the story.

No special talent is required to learn this technique. Lots of practice and patience combined with scissors and paper are the only requirements. If you have trouble following the pattern or cuts, draw light pencil marks on the paper to show you how and where to cut.

A variation on the fold-and-cut story is the paperfolding technique. Paperfolding or origami has been practiced by the Japanese for hundreds of years, and in recent years has become very popular in the U.S.

With some practice and imagination you can develop your own paper stories. There are a number of books available that contain ready-made instructions and stories for fold-and-cut stories including: *Handbook for Storytellers* by Caroline Feller Bauer; *Elementary School Library Resource Kit* by Jerry J. Mallett and Marian R. Bartch; *A Treasury of Trickster Tales, Storytellers Sampler,* and *Mystery-Fold* by Valerie Marsh; *The Story Vine* by Anne Pellowski; and *Just Enough to Make a Story* by Nancy Schimmel.

Tagboard, chalk talk, and fold-and-cut stories use inexpensive, readily available materials and can enhance any storytelling session. The discussion of stories that follows focuses on the tagboard method.

Tagboard

Dinosaur in Trouble

by Sharon Gordon
Troll Associates, 1980

Summary: Denny, the dinosaur, keeps everyone awake with his snoring until the townspeople come up with a unique solution to the problem.

Procedure: Because this book is so small, it is difficult to use with a larger group of children. By transferring the illustrations and text to large tagboard sheets, it is possible to use the story with a larger group. Because the story is so short, you might want to use it in conjunction with another story on dinosaurs or another theme. Use the first tagboard for the title, and include a picture of Denny as well as the author's name.

Materials needed:
- 12 tagboard sheets (12"x18")
- black and red markers
- opaque projector

Optional Activities

Dinosaur Coloring Sheet
Create an activity sheet that has a picture of the dinosaur on it with the town in the background. Children can color it and add more details at home.

Find the Dinosaurs (activity sheet)
Give each child a puzzle sheet on which to find and circle all the different types of dinosaurs.

Related Books: Dinosaur Tales

Donnelly, Liza. *Dinosaurs' Halloween.* New York: Scholastic, 1987. One Halloween night, a little boy goes trick-or-treating with his new friend.

Hearn, Diane Dawson. *Dad's Dinosaur Day.* New York: Macmillan, 1993. When Mikey's dad turns into a dinosaur, they have a lot of fun, but Mikey finds himself longing for his old dad back.

Marton, Rodney. *There's a Dinosaur in the Park.* Illustrated by John Siow. Milwaukee: Gareth Stevens, 1986. This is an imaginative tale of a small boy who spots a dinosaur lurking in the shadows of his favorite playground.

Morgan, Michaela. *Dinostory.* Pictures by True Kelley. New York: Dutton, 1991. When Andrew asks for a dinosaur for his birthday, he gets more than he bargained for.

Wilhelm, Hans. *Tyrone the Horrible.* New York: Scholastic, 1988. A small dinosaur named Boland discovers the best way to deal with bullies like Tyrone.

Preparation time
Story & tagboard: 10–20 min.
Optional Activities
  Dinosaur Coloring Sheet: 5–10 min.
  Find the Dinosaurs: 5–10 min.

Find the Dinosaurs

The word puzzle below contains the names of 15 different types of dinosaurs. They can be found up, down, backward and forward, and diagonally.

```
S  U  R  U  A  S  O  I  H  C  A  R  B  I
T  Y  R  A  N  N  O  S  A  U  R  U  S  C
R  D  S  D  I  P  L  O  D  O  C  U  S  H
I  G  U  A  N  O  D  O  N  S  R  R  Y  T
C  S  R  N  O  D  O  I  T  U  R  V  C  H
E  P  U  W  O  D  X  K  A  R  P  R  E  Y
R  O  A  X  C  Z  F  S  K  U  S  N  P  O
A  T  S  R  I  E  O  X  K  A  M  O  E  S
T  A  O  M  D  L  I  E  W  S  N  D  H  A
O  R  M  T  L  Z  V  O  E  O  Y  O  H  U
P  E  S  A  G  N  Z  E  O  T  F  R  S  R
S  C  A  R  K  M  Z  O  Q  N  J  T  C  U
C  O  H  S  U  R  U  A  S  O  G  E  T  S
V  T  C  L  K  E  Q  I  R  R  H  M  B  O
R  O  T  P  A  R  I  V  O  B  N  I  X  C
I  R  L  D  P  T  E  R  A  N  O  D  O  N
B  P  L  E  S  I  O  S  A  U  R  U  S  T
```

Allosaurus	Diplodocus	Protoceratops
Brachiosaurus	Ichthyosaurus	Pteranodon
Brontosaurus	Iguanodon	Stegosaurus
Chasmosaurus	Oviraptor	Triceratops
Dimetrodon	Plesiosaur	Tyrannosaurus

 Tagboard

Harold and the Purple Crayon

by Crockett Johnson
Harper and Row, 1958

Summary: Harold and his trusty purple crayon set off for some adventures in the night.

Procedure: Introduce the story by asking the children if they have ever played "make believe." Ask the group the question, "If you could pretend to be anyone and to go anywhere, what would you be and where would you go?" After discussing a few of the answers, lead into the story by saying that Harold is a little boy who does a lot of pretending along with his purple crayon.

Use the opaque projector to enlarge the illustrations from the story. For the title page, use the cover of the book and draw Harold holding his purple crayon. For the rest of the story, adapt illustrations to cover one or more pages of the text. Write the story lines that match the illustration on the back of the tagboard, and number the tagboards in sequence. As you hold up the appropriate picture, read the text from the back of the tagboard.

Materials needed:
- 22 tagboard sheets (size 12"x18")
- black and purple markers
- opaque projector

The series of illustrations from the book are transferred onto tagboard using the opaque projector. You can adapt the illustrations to cover any number of pages of story lines, for example:

- Tagboard 1—Title page
- Tagboard 2—Harold drawing the moon
- Tagboard 3—Harold drawing the path
- Tagboard 4—Harold walking

Optional Activities

Harold

After the story, give each child a coloring sheet with a picture of Harold and his crayon in one corner. The children can use their own purple crayons to create more adventures for Harold.

Materials needed:
- coloring sheets
- purple crayons

An Adventure in Colors

As a follow-up activity, give each child a sheet of blank paper. Explain that each child is to draw a picture of a boy or girl, to choose a color, and to draw an adventure for the person. Entitle the drawing "_____ and his or her __(color)__ Crayon" (for example, "Mary and her Green Crayon"). Display the drawings in the library or classroom.

Materials needed:
- drawing paper
- assorted colors of crayons

Related Books: Imaginative Trips

Keats, Ezra Jack. *Regards to the Man in the Moon.* New York: Harper and Row, 1981. Louis and his friend Susie build a spaceship from junk and take an imaginary journey to distant worlds and galaxies.

Seuss, Dr. *And to Think I Saw It on Mulberry Street.* New York: Vanguard Press, 1937. In this imaginative tale, a horse and cart turn into a circus bandwagon drawn by two giraffes and an elephant.

Tompert, Ann. *Little Fox Goes to the End of the World.* Illustrated by John C. Wallner. New York: Crown, 1976. Little Fox tells her mother how she will conquer the elements and subdue fierce animals when she goes to the end of the world.

 Preparation time
Story & tagboards: 1–2 hours
Optional Activities
    Harold: 5–10 min.
    An Adventure in Colors: 5–15 min.

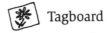 Tagboard

Harry Hoyle's Giant Jumping Bean

by William Van Horn
Atheneum, 1978

Summary: A dangerous jumping bean puts Harry Hoyle's collections in danger.

Procedure: Begin the story session by talking about collecting things. Some people collect stamps, rocks, shells, or stuffed animals. Ask the audience if anyone has a special collection of his or her own. Lead into the story by saying that Harry Hoyle is not very particular about what he collects, he just likes to collect things. As you tell the story, hold up the appropriate tagboard for the text. When you are finished with the story, have the children think of more things that Harry could collect.

Materials needed:
- 18 tagboard sheets (12"x18")
- markers
- old magazines
- scissors
- glue and/or paste

For the tagboards, use sixteen sheets for the story and illustrations. Use the other two sheets for the title page and for the words "THE END." Use a combination of illustrations from the picture book and illustrations cut from old magazines. When talking about the rooms holding Harry's collections, use pictures of marbles for one tagboard, telephones for another, and ice cream cones for a third.

Optional Activity

What Do You Collect?

Give each child a sheet of paper or lightweight cardboard. Explain that you would like for each to think of something that he or she would like to collect. The children can draw pictures of their collections or cut out and paste pictures of things on the cardboard. The collection posters can be displayed in the library or classroom.

Materials needed:
- paper or lightweight poster board
- scissors
- old magazines
- pencils, markers, and crayons
- glue or paste

Related Books: Beans and More Beans

Briggs, Raymond. *Jim and the Beanstalk.* New York: Coward, McCann and Geoghegan, 1970. It's Jim's turn to climb the beanstalk, where he meets the giant's son who turns out not to be mean and scary.

DeRegniers, Beatrice Schenk. *Jack and the Beanstalk: Retold in Verse for Boys and Girls to Read Themselves.* New York: Atheneum, 1985. This is a retelling of the old folktale of Jack and the magic beans.

Martin, Judith, and Charlip, Remy. *Jumping Beans.* New York: Knopf, 1963. When a housewife buys some red beans, the beans turn out to be a lively bunch of Mexican jumping beans.

Giveaway

Beans for everyone!

 Preparation time
Story & tagboards—45–90 min.
Optional Activities
What Do You Collect? 10–20 min.
Mosaic Turtles 10–20 min.

Tagboard

Little Blue and Little Yellow

by Leo Lionni
Astor, 1959

Summary: This story is an ingenious tale of friendship and family and two blobs of color.

Procedure: The illustrations in the book are rather small and are difficult to use with large groups. However, by recreating the pictures on tagboard, you can share the story with a large group. Introduce the tale by stating that this is the story of two best friends who are separated and manage to come together again.

Materials needed:
- 20–22 white tagboard sheets (8 1/2" x 11")
- markers

Optional Activity

What Color Is It?

Give the children sheets of heavy drawing paper, paint and paintbrushes. Explain that you are going to mix colors and create some new ones of your own. In the story, a little blue and a little yellow combined to make green, so have the children start with that combination. Give them other colors to mix and ask what the results will be. Be sure to tell the children to clean their paintbrushes thoroughly before they mix each color. You might want to demonstrate thorough cleaning.

Materials needed:
- heavy drawing paper
- paint (tempera or watercolors)
- paintbrushes
- water
- old rags
- newspapers
- smocks to cover children

Related Books: Making Colors

Emberley, Edward. *Green Says Go.* Boston: Little, Brown, 1968. This book tells all about colors—how they are made, differences in light and dark, and how to mix colors.

Lobel, Arnold. *The Great Blueness and Other Predicaments.* New York: Harper, 1968. To help brighten up a black and white world, a wizard sets out to invent colors.

Poulet, Virginia. *Blue Bug's Book of Colors.* Chicago: Children's Press, 1981. Blue Bug learns all about colors and how they are created.

Walsh, Ellen S. *Mouse Paint.* San Diego: Harcourt Brace, 1992. When they find some empty jars of paint, three little mice decide to paint themselves and everything around them.

Giveaways

Small piece of blue and yellow transparency film so children can make their own "little green," and information chart on colors

Preparation time
Story & tagboards: 1–2 hours
Optional Activities
What Color Is It? 10–25 min.

What Color Am I?

This is what happens if you mix:

yellow + blue   =   green

red + yellow   =   orange

red + blue   =   purple

black + orange =   brown

white + black   =   gray

red + white   =   pink

Now, try these and tell what happens if you mix:

red + green + white   =

white + purple   =

orange + violet   =

orange + black + yellow   =

red + yellow + blue   =

orange + green   =

red + yellow + white   =

turquoise + orange + white =

red + yellow + white   =

Try some color combinations of your own and tell what happened.

The Rose in My Garden

by Arnold Lobel

Greenwillow, 1984

Summary: This participation story is a cumulative tale of a cat and mouse frolicking in a garden of beautiful flowers.

Procedure: This cumulative tale is a good one to use in the spring, when all the flowers begin to bloom, and people are talking about gardens. Introduce the story by talking about living things that you might find in a flower garden. Before reading the story, pass out tagboard cards to children seated in the audience. Save the last tagboard for yourself. Explain to each child the type of flower or animal that he or she will hold up during the story and then move the children to the outside edges of the group. As you read the title and first line of the story, the child holding the tagboard with the rose will stand up. For the next line the child holding the bee picture will stand, and so on until you read the last line, when you will hold up the appropriate picture. The children holding the tagboards will be seated in a circle around the rest of the group until called to stand and then they will remain standing throughout the story.

After the story, hold up a real flower. Take it apart, and let the children look at the different parts. Reinforce the discussion by giving each child a fact sheet on plants and seeds.

Materials needed:
- 15 tagboard sheets (12"x18")
- colored pencils
- opaque projector

You will need fifteen tagboards, each with one of the following pictures: (1) a rose, (2) a bee, (3) hollyhocks, (4) marigolds, (5) zinnias, (6) daisies, (7) bluebells, (8) lilies, (9) peonies, (10) pansies, (11) tulips, (12) sunflowers, (13) a field mouse, (14) a cat with a tattered ear, and (15) a cat with a bandaged nose.

Optional Activities

Flower Search (activity sheet)

Using all of the flowers and characters mentioned in the story, create a find-a-hidden-word puzzle. (The "Flower Search" activity is such a word puzzle.) Include a list of the words that can be found in the puzzle. Children should circle the words when they find them.

Create Your Own Garden Collage

Using a blank sheet of cardboard and pictures, children can create a garden picture of their own. The children can cut out pictures of flowers, trees, and shrubs from old catalogs and magazines and glue the pictures on the cardboard to create a collage.

Materials needed:
- scissors
- glue or paste
- old magazines, newspaper advertisements, and seed catalogs

Where Do Flowers Grow? (activity sheet)

The activity sheet combines a connect-the-dots picture with a flower identification exercise. The children have to identify the flowers and to use the circled letters to answer the title question.

 Preparation time
Story & tagboards: 1–2 hours
Optional Activities
  Flower Search: 10–20 min.
  Create Your Own Garden Collage:
    5 min. for preparation; 15–30 min. for children to complete.
  Where Do Flowers Grow? 5–15 min.

Related Books: Gardening

Ehlert, Lois. *Planting a Rainbow.* Orlando: Harcourt Brace Jovanovich, 1988. A child describes the garden that she plants every year with her mother.

Hines, Anna Grossnickle. *Miss Emma's Wild Garden.* New York: Greenwillow, 1997. Miss Emma tells Chloe all about the wonderful things in her garden including a very special wild creature.

Stewart, Sarah. *The Gardener.* New York: Farrar, Straus & Giroux, 1997. A young girl describes the year she spends with her uncle, a cantankerous baker, and how her love of gardening helps transform the neighborhood and the lives of the people there.

Wilner, Isabel. *A Garden Alphabet.* Pictures by Asley Wolff. New York: Dutton, 1991. From A to Z, the reader learns how a garden is planned and planted, how things grow and the happiness that a garden can bring.

Giveaways

Fact sheet on plants and seeds, flower seeds, and perhaps a small milk carton filled with soil for each child

Flower Search

What can you find in the garden? Circle the words as you find them. Answers can be across, up and down, and diagonally.

```
S  D  L  O  G  I  R  A  M  T  E
U  D  W  I  L  V  P  W  M  W  Z
N  A  L  R  Q  Y  E  T  N  B  A
F  I  E  L  D  M  O  U  S  E  T
L  S  C  C  I  Y  N  L  K  A  O
O  I  S  M  V  R  I  I  C  U  P
W  E  E  L  G  T  E  P  O  N  X
E  S  I  L  A  X  S  S  H  P  U
R  P  L  Z  R  R  E  B  Y  A  P
D  F  I  A  D  L  W  I  L  N  E
Y  B  L  U  E  B  E  L  L  S  O
V  Z  I  N  N  I  A  S  O  I  Y
O  E  I  N  V  W  E  R  H  E  H
U  R  T  N  C  B  H  O  I  S  P
```

bluebells	pansies
cat	peonies
daisies	rose
field mouse	sunflower
hollyhocks	tulips
lilies	zinnias
marigolds	

Where Do These Flowers Grow?

Using the words below identify each of the flowers. Transfer the circled letters to the bottom line to discover "Where do these flowers grow?"

rose   tulips   marigold   peony   lilies   daisy   pansy

1. _ _ _ _ ◯ _ _ _

2. _ ◯ _ _ _ _

3. ◯ _ _ _ _

4. ◯ _ _ _ _

5. _ _ _ _ ◯ _ _

6. _ _ _ ◯ _ _

7. _ _ _ _ _ ◯

ANSWER:

_ _ _ _ _ _ _ _ _ _ _ _ _ _ _

About Plants and Seeds

The Parts of a Plant

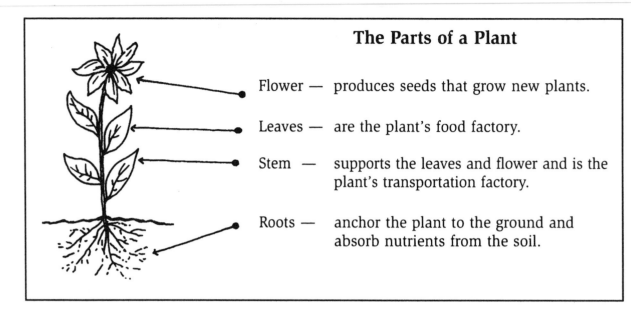

Flower — produces seeds that grow new plants.

Leaves — are the plant's food factory.

Stem — supports the leaves and flower and is the plant's transportation factory.

Roots — anchor the plant to the ground and absorb nutrients from the soil.

 ## How Seeds Travel

- Some plants scatter their own seeds by popping the seeds out when ripe.

- The wind scatters seeds.

- Hitchhiking–some seeds cling to an animal's fur, an insect's body or a person's clothing.

- By water.

- Man carries seeds by planting.

- Birds and animals carry seeds. Sometimes the seeds that animals eat pass through their bodies.

Types of Flowers

Annuals — live only a year or so and come from seeds (such as pansies).

Perennials — grow back every year and come from seeds, or from dividing bigger plants (examples are lilies and peonies). Some perennials, such as tulips, come from bulbs.

Wildflowers — grow almost everywhere and come from seeds scattered by nature (for example, daisies or dandelions).

Tagboard

The Silly Goose

by Jack Kent
Prentice-Hall, 1983

Summary: The fox and the goose go jogging in the woods and encounter several dangerous situations, but they manage to finish their jog intact.

Procedure: The simple illustrations and clear-cut action make this a good story to use on tagboard. Copy the actual story on the back of the appropriate piece of tagboard so that you can read the story (or plot) as the corresponding tagboard is shown. The illustrations could be shown and the plot unfold as follows:

1. Title of story and author.
2. Illustration of the goose jogging along in the woods.
3. Trees—with goose and fox jogging.
4. Tree on top of the fox, with the goose standing on the fallen tree.
5. The goose digging a hole under the fox.
6. The goose stopping his jogging, with the fox continuing toward the crocodile's open mouth.
7. The goose and the crocodile (fox inside crocodile's mouth). (At this point, you can pull out a feather taped to the back of the tagboard to use to tickle the crocodile's nose.)
8. The goose, the fox, and the eagle.
9. The goose standing on the ground, while the fox is being carried away by the eagle.
10. The goose landing on the eagle who drops the fox.
11. The fox and the goose jogging in the woods.
12. The goose shoving the fox in a hole and throwing leaves on him.
13. A hunting party passing by the goose standing over the fox in the hole covered by leaves.

Materials needed:
- 13 tagboard sheets (12"x18")
- yellow, brown, green, red, and black markers
- opaque projector

Draw the appropriate characters on sheets of tagboard. Using a black marker, write the story lines on each sheet of tagboard.

Optional Activities

Silly Goose
Trace a picture of the Silly Goose onto a piece of paper. Make enough copies for each child to have one. The children can color the picture and give the goose more adventures of her own.

Who Saved the Fox? (activity sheet)
Give each child an activity sheet containing a dot-to-dot picture.

Related Books: What Goose Is This?

Bang, Molly. *Goose.* New York: Blue Sky, 1996. When an egg rolls in their nest, a family of woodchucks raise the goose that hatches.

Duvoisin, Roger. *Petunia.* New York: Knopf, 1950. When Petunia gives all the other farm animals advice, she creates more problems than she solves.

Pilkey, Dav. *The Silly Gooses.* New York: Blue Sky, 1997. this is the story of the silliest family of geese that ever flew—in a hot air balloon.

Simont, Marc. *The Goose That Almost Got Cooked.* New York: Scholastic, 1997. A goose settles on a farm where life is very pleasant until she discovers the real reason that the farmer keeps geese.

 Preparation time
Story & tagboards: 30–45 min.
Optional Activities
Silly Goose: 5–10 min.
Who Saved the Fox: 5–10 min.

Who Saved the Fox?

Connect the dots 1 thru 28 and discover: Who saved the Fox?

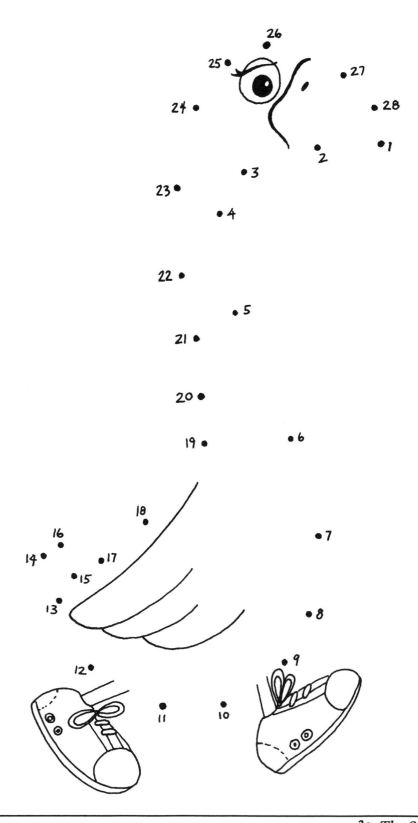

 Tagboard

This Is the Bread I Baked for Ned

By Crescent Dragonwagon • Illustrated by Isadore Seltzer
Macmillan, 1989

Summary: Glenda spends the day making a delicious meal for Ned, only to be surprised when he brings home lots of friends and pets.

Procedures: Begin the story session by asking the children to describe a very special meal that someone has made for them. Talk about favorite foods and how they make us feel. Lead into the story by saying that Glenda spends the day making a special meal for Ned, but things don't turn out the way that she planned. Draw freehand illustrations for this story on tagboard. The text can be written on the back of the tagboards.

Illustrations should include:
1. Glenda holding a platter of bread.
2. A round of cheese on a cutting board.
3. A bowl of salad greens.
4. A vinegar crock.
5. A bowl of olive oil.
6. Olives on a plate.
7. A tureen of soup.
8. A bouquet of tulips in a crock.
9. Two plates and soup bowls.
10. A group of people at the door.
11. Ned washing dishes.
12. Nighttime and open window with a crescent moon and stars shining.

Optional Activities

What's for Dinner?
Divide the children into groups of two to four and have the children write their own cumulative tale about a special dinner. Brainstorm ideas based on the discussion that took place before the story and write a tale about the special meal. Be sure that the children include at least six items in their cumulative tale. After writing the tale, then illustrate it on sheets of tagboard and write the text on the back. The illustrations can be drawn by hand or cut out from old magazines.

Materials needed:
• tagboard
• paper
• pencils
• coloring medium
• old magazines (optional)
• scissors (optional)
• glue (optional)

Related Books: More Food Tales

Grossman, Bill. *My Little Sister Ate One Hare.* Illustrations by Kevin Hawkes. New York: Crown, 1996. Little sister eats a variety of delicacies including bats, shrews, and ants.

Kimmel, Eric A. *The Gingerbread Man.* Art by Meagan Lloyd. New York: Holiday House, 1993. This is the classic tale of everyone chasing the gingerbread man.

Polacco, Patricia. *In Enzo's Splendid Gardens.* New York: Philomel, 1997. A wild and crazy bee creates chaos in an outdoor restaurant.

Robard, Rose. *The Cake That Mack Ate.* Illustrations by Maryann Kovalski. Boston: Little, Brown, 1987. A happy dog devours all the ingredients that go into the cake and then the cake itself.

Giveaways
Bread and soup

 Preparation time
Story: 10–20 min.
Optional Activities
What's for Dinner? 10–30 min.

This Is the Place

By Joanna Cole • Illustrated by William Van Horn
Scholastic, 1986

Summary: When Monty, the bear, keeps breaking things in his house, he decides to find a new and bigger house, only to discover that his task is not an easy one to accomplish.

Procedure: Introduce the story by saying that sometimes people are not satisfied with the things they have. Then, discuss the fact that Monty, the bear in the story, wants a bigger house but that finding one proves to be a bigger problem than he thought it would be. Use tagboard to read the story to the children. You will need approximately twelve tagboard sheets to present the story. Use the opaque projector or draw the illustrations freehand on the tagboard. Write the appropriate story line on the backs of the tagboards. Many of the scenes will be of the different houses that Monty finds on his trip. For those scenes, you can use a cardboard cutout of Monty that can be attached and removed from the tagboard.

Materials needed:
- 12 white tagboard sheets (12"x18")
- colored markers
- scissors
- masking tape (to attach and remove Monty)
- opaque projector

You will need to make the following tagboard sheets:

1. Title page with cardboard cutout of Monty attached As you read the title and author, remove Monty from the title page to use later in the story.
2. An inside view of Monty's original house with things broken
3. A cave with a dragon inside it
4. Monty with his pants on fire
5. The candy house
6. A scene of the ground with the candy house gone
7. A houseboat on the water
8. Monty inside the tepee
9. A thin house
10. A scary house
11. Monty walking through the woods (disheartened about his search)
12. An outside shot of Monty's original house

Attach the cardboard cutout of Monty to tagboards 2, 3, 5, 6, 7, 9, 10, and 12 as you read the part of the story that corresponds to the board being shown.

Optional Activity

Find a House for Monty (activity sheet)
This is a simple activity sheet for the children. The sheet has paw prints leading across the bottom of the page. The children are to draw a new house for Monty.

Related Books: A New Home

Barrett, Judith. *Old MacDonald Had an Apartment House.* Illustrated by Ron Barrett. New York: Atheneum, 1969. Old MacDonald, the building supervisor, turns the apartment building into an indoor farm.

Burton, Virginia. *The Little House.* Boston: Houghton Mifflin, 1942. A country house is unhappy as the city surrounds it with noise and traffic.

Hoff, Syd. *Grizzwold.* New York: Harper and Row, 1963. After the lumbermen destroy his home, the likable bear Grizzwold searches for a new one.

Simmonds, Posy. *F–Freezing ABC.* New York: Knopf, 1995. The anteater, bear, cat, and duck search for a new home that is warm and safe from the winter weather.

Preparation time
Story & tagboards: 45–60 min.
Optional Activities
Find a House for Monty: 5–10 min.

Find a House for Monty

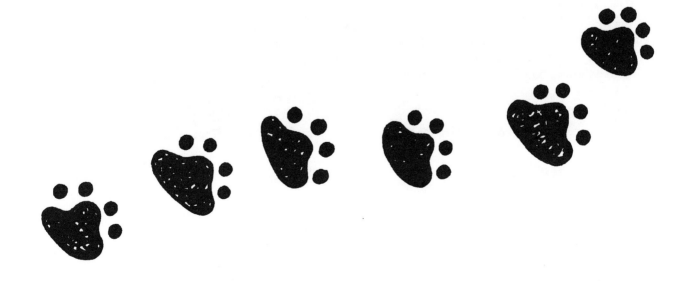

Technology & Storytelling

At first glance, it may not appear that using technology would have much to do with the traditional art of storytelling. However, technological tools can be used in a variety of ways to enhance a storytelling session. Computers, scanners, and digital cameras can be used to create storytelling props and extension projects. Overhead and opaque projectors are useful for making puppet characters and for presenting shadow puppet shows. A computer and Internet connection can provide a storyteller with unlimited communication through email, listservs, online stories and resources to use, and updates on conferences, workshops, and other projects occurring around the world.

The Internet is a wonderful resource for all kinds of materials, and it is an excellent source for locating stories and storytellers. There are literally hundreds of sites that provide information for both veteran and rookie storytellers. One very important factor to remember in using resources from the Internet is to always attribute the source. It is very easy to download information, and it would not be proper to omit citing the source of the material you are using.

Storytelling

Storynet is the official Web site for the National Storytelling Association, located in Jonesborough, Tennessee. Their site lists storytelling events, links to other sites of value to storytellers, an online store of publications, a chatroom, a directory of members, and information the the NSA.

http://www.storynet.org (*Verified 8/20/98*)

The Storytelling Ring is a storytelling resource that is sponsored by WebRing, a network of member sites and commercial sponsors. This resource allows you to visit other sites on the Web that are dedicated to the art of storytelling. Each is connected to the other in a daisy-chained ring allowing you to go from one to the other and finally back to the first by pressing the NEXT button on each site. The ring includes over 50 sites and continues to grow.

http://www.tiac.net/users/papajoe/ring.htm (*Verified 8/20/98*)

The Storytelling FAQ If you are looking for information about storytelling organizations, professional storytellers or answers to questions, the first and best site to hit is The Storytelling FAQ. It includes extensive information about copyright laws, storytelling magazines, organizations, ongoing workshops, conferences and events, and notable storytellers. The site is maintained by Tim Sheppard, a publisher who specializes in miniature books, (e-mail: tim@lilliput-p.win-uk) or write to 10 Manor Rd., Bishopton, Bristol BS7 8PY, England.

http://www.lilliput.co.uk (*Verified 8/20/98*)

The Art of Storytelling is a Web site devoted to storytelling techniques, storytellers and associations, and many links to story sources. The articles and links to storytelling basics and techniques are very good for the beginner and the veteran storyteller. The site is maintained and sponsored by Eldrbarry, an online bookstore specializing in storytelling resources.

http://www.seanet.com/~eldrbarry/roos/art.htm (*Verified 8/20/98*)

Handbook for Storytellers A very comprehensive online *Handbook for Storytellers* was prepared by Inez Ramsey, a member of the John Marshall University faculty. It offers information on the history of storytelling, how to choose and tell your story, and an extensive bibliography.

http://falcon.jmu.edu/~ramseyil/storyhandbook.htm (*Verified 8/20/98*)

Aaron's Storytelling Page is a good source for information on telling, picking, and preparing a story. There is a great deal of practical information for storytellers including a list of professional resources. This Web site is maintained and sponsored by children's author Aaron Shepard.

http://www.aaronshep.com/storytelling/
(Verified 8/20/98)

Cheesecake's Storytelling Pages is a comprehensive resource site for the performance and variety artist. It also includes a section on storytelling with numerous links, a calendar of events, and a list of vendors. The sponsor is Clown Supplies, Inc.

http://CheesecakeAndFriends.com/stories.asp
(Verified 8/20/98)

Better Kid Care: Storytelling is part of the Better Kids Care Project posted by the Pennsylvania State University Cooperative Extension. This page provides some very basic guidelines about the oral tradition of storytelling and different ways to tell stories. It includes techniques, titles of stories to tell and extension activities.

http://www.nncc.org/Curriculum/better.storytell.
html   *(Verified 8/20/98)*

Flannelboard

Good Internet sites on using the flannelboard are not very plentiful, but there are a few that offer some basic advice.

Storytelling with the Flannelboard is a good site for basic how-tos and resources. Information on making and storing flannelboard materials, choosing stories, and a bibliography of resources are included. Information used on the site was compiled from various sources by Inez Ramsey, who is on the faculty of John Marshall University.

http://raven.jmu.edu/~ramseyil/flannel2.htm
(Verified 8/20/98)

Flannelboard is another simple basic guide to using flannelboards. It includes a list of professional resources, how to make flannelboard characters, and a nice list of stories that are good to adapt for the flannelboard. The site is maintained by the Children's Serv. Consultant of the Vermont Dept. of Libraries.

http://dol.state.vt.us/gopher_root5/libraries/cbec
/flanlbrd.lis   *(Verified 8/20/98)*

Puppetry

The Puppetry Home Page is a collection of articles, history, classified ads and related information. It includes a link to classified ads for puppet troupes, puppet builders, puppets, and even places to perform. Links to other puppet resources include puppetry organizations, festivals, theaters, schools, exhibits, builders, performers, newsgroups, and chatrooms. The wealth of information and frequently updated links to puppetry resources on the Web make this one of the most valuable resources on the Internet about puppetry. The site was developed and is maintained by Rose Sage of Sagecraft Inc.

http://www.sagecraft.com/puppetry   *(Verified 8/20/98)*

On-Line Puppet Theater offers a catalog to puppets and books, tips for puppeteers, an online theater, paper puppets and patterns to download and make with kids, and links to puppetry resources. The section on scrap puppets and patterns is especially useful for storytellers who plan extension activities after a storytelling session. It also provides a source for children to publish plays and rhymes they have written for use with puppets or other theater. Stage Hand Puppets, a publisher and supplies devoted to puppetry located in Nova Scotia, is the sponsor of this Web site.

http://www3.ns.sympatico.ca/onstage/puppets/
(Verified 8/20/98)

The Muppets Home Page is a popular site to use with younger children. It includes an extensive gallery of famous puppets and many hot links to other puppet pages. This site is sponsored and maintained by the Jim Henson Co.

http://www.muppets.com *(Verified 8/20/98)*

Puppetools is an excellent source for product information, research articles on the value and use of puppets, and even pictures of puppets that children have made. The site includes an excellent list of links to more online puppet resources. Puppetools, a publisher of puppetry resources and supplier of puppetry resources maintains and sponsors this site.

http://www.puppetools.com *(Verified 8/20/98)*

Read-Aloud

Jed's Guide to Story Reading offers advice on starting and maintaining story reading groups. Ideas about planning a reading, scheduling, and even choosing a story are discussed in some detail. This resource was developed by Jed Hartman, an independent writer with an interest in storytelling.

http://kith.org/logos/things/reading.html
(Verified 8/20/98)

Other Resources

Storytell is a mailing list hosted by Texas Women's University that reaches storytellers around the world. Messages and discussions about sources, venues, ethics, and other storytelling topics are part of Storytell. To subscribe, send email to STORYTEL-REQUEST@venus.twu.edu. The message should read SUBSCRIBE STORYTELL.

Alt.arts.storytelling is a newsgroup devoted to discussions of the oral tradition of storytelling, not the art of writing stories.

Storyteller.net is a commercial site devoted to providing storytellers with an outlet to post their personal pages, audio files of stories being told, email, and discussions about storytelling.

These Web sites are only an introduction to the many resources that exist on the Internet. The number and type of sites changes constantly, so it is important to regularly review the materials available.

Bibliography

General References

Anderson, Paul S. *Storytelling with the Flannel Board: Book Two.* 2nd ed. Minneapolis: Denison, 1985.

Armour, Maureen W. *Poetry, The Magic Language Children Learn to Read and Write It.* Englewood, CO: Teacher Ideas, 1994.

Baker, Augusta, and Ellin Greene. *Storytelling Art and Technique,* 3rd ed. New York: Bowker, 1996.

Baker, Augusta, and Ellin Greene. "Storytelling: Preparation and Presentation, " *School Library Journal,* (March 1978), pp. 93–96.

Baltuck, Naomi. *Crazy Gibberish and Other Story Hour Stretches.* Hamden, Conn.: Linnet, 1993.

Bannister, Barbara F. *The New Elementary School Librarian's Almanac: A Complete Media Program for Every Month of the School Year.* West Nyack, NY: Center for Applied Research, 1991.

Barton, Bob. *Tell Me Another.* Markham, Ontario: Pembroke, 1986.

Barton, Bob, and David Booth. *Stories In the Classroom.* Markham, Ontario: Pembroke, 1990.

Bauer, Carolyn. *Carolyn Feller Bauer's New Handbook for Storytellers: With Stories, Poems, Magic and More.* Chicago: American Library Association, 1993.

———. *Celebrations: Read-Aloud Holiday and Theme Book Programs.* New York: H. W. Wilson, 1985.

———. *Leading to Books Through Puppets.* Chicago: American Library Association, 1997.

———. *This Way to Books.* New York: H. W. Wilson, 1983.

Bay, Jeanette. *A Treasury of Flannelboard Stories.* Fort Atkinson, WI: Alleyside, 1995.

Beatty, Janice J. *Picture Book Storytelling.* Ft. Worth, TX: Harcourt Brace, 1994.

Bonnell, Cathy C. "Vacation Fun in the School Library," *School Library Journal,* (January 1985), pp. 24–26.

Borba, Michele, and Dan Ungaro. *Bookends Activities, Centers, Contracts, and Ideas Galore to Enhance Children's Literature.* Carthage, Ill.: Good Apple, 1982.

Breneman, Lucille N., and Bren Breneman. *Once Upon a Time: A Storytelling Handbook.* Chicago: Nelson-Hall, 1983.

Cassidy, Marshall. *Storytelling Step-by-Step.* San Jose, CA: Resource Publ., 1990.

Chadwick, Roxane. *Felt Board Story Times.* Ft. Atkinson, WI: Alleyside, 1997.

Champlin, Connie, and Nancy Renfro. *Storytelling with Puppets.* 2nd ed. Chicago: American Library Association, 1997.

Chepesiuk, Ron. "Special Report: A Master Storyteller," *Wilson Library Bulletin,* (May 1986), pp. 28–29.

Cole, Joanna, and Calmensen, Stephanie, comp. *The Read-Aloud Treasury.* New York: Doubleday, 1988.

Cullum, Carolyn N. *The Storytime Sourcebook: A Compendium of Ideas and Resources for Storytellers.* New York: Neal-Schuman, 1990.

Davis, Donald D. *Telling Your Own Stories: For Family and Classroom Storytelling.* Little Rock: August House, 1993.

Druce, Arden. *Chalk Talk Stories.* Metuchen, NJ: Scarecrow, 1993.

Emmens, Carol A. "Storyhours in Cable TV," *School Library Journal,* (March 1985), p. 126.

Fader, Daniel. *The New Hooked on Books.* New York: Berkeley, 1982.

Freeman, Judy. *More Books Kids Will Sit Still For: A Read-Aloud Guide.* New York: Bowker, 1995.

Gillespie, John T., and Corinne J. Naden. eds. *Best Books for Children Preschool Through Grade 6.* 6th ed. New York: Bowker, 1998.

Greene, Ellin. "There Are No Talent Scouts," *School Library Journal*, (November 1982), pp. 25–27.

Guerrier, Charlie. *A Collage of Crafts*. New York: Tichnor & Fields, 1994.

Hamilton, Leslie. *Child's Play: 200 Instant Crafts and Activities for Preschoolers*. New York: Crown, 1989.

Holden, Susan, and Carol Albano. "Do You Have a Knack for Storytelling?" *School Library Journal*, (October 1987), p. 50.

Irving, Jan, and Robin Currie. *Full Speed Ahead! Stories and Activities for Children on Transportation*. Littleton, Colo.: Libraries Unlimited, 1989.

———. *Mudluscious: Stories and Activities Featuring Food for Preschool Children*. Littleton, Colo.: Libraries Unlimited, 1986.

Jalongo, Mary Renck, and Renck, Melissa Ann. "Stories that Sing: A Storytime Resource," *School Library Journal*, (September 1985), pp. 42–43.

Keeler, Kathleen. "Making Picture Books Come Alive," *School Library Journal*, (May 1989), p. 49.

Kimmel, Margaret Mary, and Elizabeth Segel. *For Reading Out Loud! A Guide to Sharing Books with Children*, rev. edition. New York: Dell, 1991.

Kinghorn, Harriet, and Mary Pelton. *Every Child a Storyteller: Handbook of Ideas*. Englewood, CO: Teacher Ideas, 1991.

Kinney, Jan. "Tricks of the Trade Books," *School Library Journal*, (April 1989), p. 47.

Kladder, Jeri. *Story Hours: 55 Preschool Programs for Public Libraries*. Jefferson, NC: McFarland, 1995.

Laughlin, Mildred Knight, and Letty S. Watt, *Developing Learning Skills Through Children's Literature: An Idea Book for K–5 Classrooms and Libraries*. Phoenix: Oryx Press, 1986.

Laughlin, Mildred Knight, and Patricia Payne Kardaliff. *Literature-Based Social Studies: Children's Books and Activities to Enrich the K-5 Curriculum*. Phoenix: Oryx Press, 1996.

Liebermann, Lillian. *ABC Folder Games: Patterns for Easy-to-Do Reading Games*. Palo Alto, CA: Monday Morning Books, 1991.

Lima, Carolyn W., and John A. Lima. *A to Zoo: Subject Access to Children's Picture Books*. 5th ed. New York: Bowker, 1998.

Livo, Norma J., and Sandra A. Rietz. Storytelling Activities. Littleton, Colo.: Libraries Unlimited, 1987.

McCormack, Joe. "On the Road With a Puppet Story Caravan." *School Library Journal*, (February 1985), pp. 29–31.

MacDonald, Margaret Read. *The Parents Guide to Storytelling*. New York: HarperCollins, 1995.

MacDonald, Margaret Read. *Twenty Tellable Tales*. New York: H. W. Wilson, 1991.

MacDonald, Margaret Read. *When the Lights Go Out: Twenty Scary Stories to Tell*. New York: H. W. Wilson, 1988.

Mallett, Jerry J., and Bartch, Marian R. *Elementary School Library Resource Kit*. West. Nyack, NY: Center for Applied Research, 1984.

Marsh, Valerie. *Mystery-Fold: Stories to Tell, Draw, and Fold*. Ft. Atkinson, WI: Alleyside, 1996.

———. *A Storyteller's Sampler*. Ft. Atkinson, WI: Alleyside, 1996.

———. *Terrific Tales to Tell*. Ft. Atkinson, WI: Alleyside, 1997.

McElmeel, Sharron L. *Literature Frameworks—From Apples to Zoos*. Worthington, OH: Linworth, 1997.

Mellon, Constance. "Storyteller or Performer? You Can't Tell the Difference Without a Scorecard," *School Library Journal*, (October 1986), p. 122.

Morris, Eileen, and Stephanie Pereau Crilly. *Get Ready, Set, Grow! A Preplanned Calendar of Preschool Activities*. Belmont, Calif.: David S. Lake, 1984.

Nichols, Judy. *Storytimes for Two-Year Olds*. 2nd ed. Chicago: American Library Association, 1998.

Oldfield, Margaret. *Lots More Tell and Draw Stories*. Minneapolis: Creative Storytime, 1973.

———. *More Tell and Draw Stories*. Minneapolis: Creative Storytime, 1973.

Painter, William M. "Horsin' Around with Dogs and Rabbits," *School Library Journal*, (May 1986), p. 46.

———. *Story Hours With Puppets and Other Props*. Hamden, Conn.: Library Professional Publ., 1990.

———. *Storytelling With Music, Puppets and Arts for Libraries and Classrooms*. Hamden, Conn.: Library Professional Publ., 1990.

Paulin, Mary Ann. *Creative Uses of Children's Literature.* Hamden, Conn.: Library Professional Publ., 1997.

Pellowski, Anne. *The Family Storytelling Handbook: How to Use Stories, Anecdotes, Rhymes, Handkerchiefs, Paper, and Other Objects to Enrich Your Family Traditions.* New York: Macmillan, 1987.

———. *The Story Vine: A Source Book of Unusual and Easy-to-Tell Stories from Around the World.* New York: Macmillan, 1984.

———. *The Storytelling Handbook: A Young People's Collection of Unusual Tales and Helpful Hints on How to Tell Them.* New York: Simon & Schuster, 1995.

Perry, Phyllis J. *Reading Activities & Resources That Work.* Ft. Atkinson, WI: Highsmith Press, 1997.

Peterson, Carolyn Sue, and Benny Hall. *Story Programs: A Source Book of Materials.* Metuchen, NJ: Scarecrow Books, 1980.

Pflomm, Phyllis Noe. *Chalk in Hand: The Draw and Tell Book.* Metuchen, NJ: Scarecrow Press, 1986.

Reading Rainbow Teacher's Guide: Programs 1–30. Lincoln, Neb.: Great Plains National Instructional Television Library, 1986.

Reading Rainbow Teacher's Guide Programs 31–50. Lincoln, Neb.: Great Plains National Instructional Television Library, 1988.

Reed, Barbara. "Storytelling: What It Can Teach," *School Library Journal,* (October 1987), pp. 35–39.

Sawyer, Ruth. *The Way of the Storyteller.* New York: Penguin, 1987.

Schimmel, Nancy. *Just Enough to Make a Story: A Sourcebook for Storytelling,* 3rd ed. Berkeley: Sisters' Choice, 1992.

Shapiro, Carol R. "Teaching Storytelling to Children," *School Library Journal,* (November 1984), p. 78.

Shelley, Marshall. *Telling Stories to Children.* Batavia, Ill.: Lion Publ., 1990.

Sherman, Louise. "Have a Story Lunch," *School Library Journal,* (October 1986), pp. 120–21.

Sierra, Judy. *The Flannel Board Storytelling Book.* 2nd ed. New York: Wilson, 1997.

Sierra, Judy, and Robert Kaminski. *Multicultural Folktales: Stories to Tell Young Children.* Phoenix: Oryx, 1991.

———. *Twice Upon a Time: Stories to Tell, Retell, Act Out, and Write About.* New York: H. W. Wilson, 1989.

Sitarz, Paula Gaj. *Picture Book Story Hours: From Birthdays to Bears.* Littleton, Colo.: Libraries Unlimited, 1987.

Spagnoli, Cathy. *A Treasury of Asian Stories & Activities.* Ft. Atkinson, WI: Alleyside, 1998.

Stangl, Jean. *Is Your Storytale Dragging.* Belmont, CA: Fearon, 1989.

Stewart, Barbara Home. "Folktellers '89," *School Library Journal,* (January 1989), pp. 17–23.

"Storytelling Experiment." *Library Journal,* (May 15, 1973), p. 1659.

Sutherland, Zena. *Children and Books.* 9th ed. New York: Longman, 1997.

Sutton, Roger. "Telling Tales to YA's," *School Library Journal,* (November 1983), p. 44.

Swanson, Barbara. "Participation Storytelling," *School Library Journal,* (April 1985), p. 48.

Tales As Tools: The Power of Story in the Classroom. Jonesborough, TN: National Storytelling Press, 1994.

Taylor, Prudence. "Puppets—Perennial Favorites," *School Library Journal,* (February 1985), pp. 31–33.

Theme-a-saurus. Everett, Wash.: Warren, 1989.

Totten, Kathryn. *Storytime Crafts.* Ft. Atkinson, WI: Alleyside, 1998.

Trelease, Jim. *The Read-Aloud Handbook,* rev. ed. Madison, WI: Turtleback, 1995.

Wendelin, Karla Hawkins. *Storybook Classrooms: Using Children's Literature in the Learning Center.* Atlanta: Humanities Publishing, 1987.

Wilmes, Liz, and Dick Wilmes. *Everyday Circle Times.* Dundee, Ill.: Building Blocks, 1997.

Wilson, George, and Joyce Moss. *Books for Children to Read Alone: A Guide for Parents and Librarians.* New York: Bowker, 1988.

Ziskind, Sylvia. *Telling Stories to Children.* New York: H. W. Wilson, 1976.

Puppetry Bibliography

Barr, Marilyn G. *ABC Puppets: Patterns for Cut and Paste Projects*. Palo Alto, Calif.: Monday Morning Books, 1989.

Baumgardner, Jeannette Mahan. *60 Art Projects for Children: Painting, Clay, Puppets, Prints, Masks, and More*. New York: Clarkson Potter, 1993.

Bradshaw, Cara. *Pint-Sized Puppets and Poems*. Carthage, Ill.: Good Apple, 1994.

Brady, Martha. *Artstarts: Drama, Music, Movement, Puppetry and Storytelling Activities*. Englewood, Colo.: Teacher Ideas, 1994

Buchwald, Clair. *The Puppet Book: How to Make and Operate Puppets and Stage a Puppet Play*. Boston: Plays, Inc., 1990.

Dean, Audrey Vincente. *Puppets That Are Different*. New York: Taplinger, 1974.

Engler, Larry, and Carol Fijan. *Making Puppets Come Alive: How To Learn and Teach Hand Puppetry*. New York: Dover, 1997.

Fling, Helen. *Marionettes: How To Make and Work Them*. New York: Dover, 1973.

Flower, Cedric, and Alan Jon Fortney. *Puppets: Methods and Materials*. Palo Alto, Calif.: Davis, 1983.

Forte, Imogene. *Puppet Factory*. Nashville, Tenn.: Incentive, 1984

Feericks, Mary, and Joyce Segal. *Creative Puppetry in the Classroom*. Bethel, Conn.: New Plays, 1980.

Frazier, Nancy, and Nancy Renfro. *Imagination: At Play With Puppets and Creative Drama*. Austin: Nancy Renfro Studios, 1987.

Highlights for Children, eds. *The Big Book of Things to Make and Play With: Toys, Games, Puppets*. Honesdale, PA Boyds Mills Press, 1995.

Hunt, Tamara, and Nancy Renfro. *Puppetry in Early Childhood Education*. Austin: Nancy Renfro Studios, 1982.

Jones, Candy, and Lea McGee. *Showkits: Whole Language Activities: Patterns for Making Puppets, Costumes to Use with Picture Book Characters*. Palo Alto, Calif.: Monday Morning Books, 1991.

Krisvoy, Juel. *The Good Apple Puppet Book*. Carthage, Ill.: Good Apple, 1981.

Lohnes, Marilyn. *Finger Folk*. Fort Atkinson, Wisc.: Alleyside, 1999.

Long, Teddy Cameron. *Make Your Own Performing Puppets*. New York: Sterling, 1995.

Mahlmann, Lewis, and David Cadwalader. *Plays for Your Puppeteers: 25 Puppet Plays for Easy Performances*. Boston: Plays, 1993.

Marsh, Valerie. *Puppet Tales*. Fort Atkinson, Wisc.: Alleyside Press, 1998.

McNiven, Helen and Peter. *Puppets*. New York: Thomson Learning, 1994.

Murray, Beth, ed. *Puppet and Theater Activities: Theatrical Things to Do and Make*. Honesdale, Penn.: Boyds Mills, 1995.

Painter, William M. *Storytelling With Music, Puppets and Arts for Libraries and Classrooms*. North Haven, Conn.: Library Professional Publ., 1994.

Painter, William M. *Story Hours With Puppets and Other Props*. Hamden, Conn.: Library Professional Publ., 1990.

Pflomm, Phyllis Noe. *Puppet Plays Plus: Hand Puppet Plays for Two Puppeteers*. Metuchen, NJ: Scarecrow, 1994.

Robson, Denny, and Vanessa Bailey. *Puppets*. New York: Gloucester, 1991.

Robson, Denny and Vanessa Bailey. *Shadow Theater*. New York: Gloucester Press, 1991.

Ross, Laura. *Hand Puppets: How To Make and Use Them*. New York: Dover, 1990.

Rump, Nan. *Puppets and Masks*. Worcester, Mass.: Davis, 1996.

Shelton, Julie Catherine. *Puppets, Poems & Songs*. Carthage, Ill.: Fearon, 1993.

Sierra, Judy. *Fantastic Theater: Puppets and Plays for Young Performers and Young Audiences*. New York: H.W. Wilson, 1991.

Sims, Judy. *Puppets for Dreaming and Scheming: More Than 80 Ideas for Puppet Projects*. Walnut Creek, Calif.: Learning Works, 1998.

Stregenga, Susan J. *Christian Crafts Paper Bag Puppets*. Carthage, Ill.: Shining Star, 1990.

Van Schuyver, Jan M. *Storytelling Made Easy With Puppets*. Phoenix: Oryx Press, 1995.

Wallace, Mary. *I Can Make Puppets*. Toronto: Greey de Pencier, 1994.

Watson, N. Cameron. *The Little Pigs' Puppet Book*. Boston: Little, Brown, 1990.

Wright, Lyndie. *Puppets*. New York: Franklin Watts, 1989.